In many ways, we have had the privilege of watching this book being birthed in the very heart and soul of our friend and co-laborer, Patty Juster. As a wife, a mother, and especially a lover of Israel, Patty writes out of the cry of her own soul.

As you read *The Cry*, you will weep, smile, be inspired, but most importantly you too, will experience the powerful cry of His Spirit groaning from deep within you: "Your Kingdom come on earth as it is in heaven."

—Charles and Dotty Schmitt,
Founding Pastors of Immanuel's Church and
Immanuel's Missions

When reading *The Cry*, I was deeply touched by its depth, and I knew right from the start that this was a jewel for intercessors. It is all based on the Scriptures. Patty Juster writes with in-depth wisdom and knowledge, so that while reading, one is already praying! It makes your heart long for preparing the way for the coming of our great King in Glory.

—Ans Leitner,
co-ordinator of TJCII intercessory groups in Europe

THE CRY

Patricia Juster

THE CRY

To Rend the Heavens,
Release Grace, and
Prepare the Way
of the Lord

Foreword by Jane Hansen Hoyt
President/CEO of Aglow International

TATE PUBLISHING & *Enterprises*

Published by Tate Publishing & Enterprises, LLC
127 E. Trade Center Terrace | Mustang, Oklahoma 73064 USA
1.888.361.9473 | www.tatepublishing.com

Tate Publishing is committed to excellence in the publishing industry. The company reflects the philosophy established by the founders, based on Psalm 68:11,
"The Lord gave the word and great was the company of those who published it."

Book design copyright © 2010 by Tate Publishing, LLC. All rights reserved.
Cover design by Chris Webb
Interior design by Nathan Harmony
Edited by Edie Veach

Published in the United States of America

ISBN: 978-1-61739-008-1
1. Religion / Christian Life / Spiritual Growth
2. Religion / Christian Ministry / Evangelism
10.09.03

DEDICATION

This book is dedicated to my spiritual mom and mentor, Nan Connor. Through her example of unfailing love and endurance through her own personal adversities she taught me the cry of intercession. Again and again I witnessed the response of God to her cries as a widow. I saw people come from afar to help her fix the roof of her farmhouse, mow her large yard, take care of her horses, remodel her house and give money so she can go on vacation. Truly she exemplified this scripture:

> The widow who is really in need and left all alone puts her hope in God and continues night and day to pray and to ask God for help.
>
> I Timothy 5:5

She freely gave of her love and opened her home to the needy, some of the neediest being leaders in the church world who needed the spoiling love of a mother's cooking and unconditional hugs. She walked with me through every step of the way as I journeyed through my valley of the shadow of death. Together we knelt before her sofa and cried out to God for answers and found comfort and help in my time of greatest need.

TABLE OF CONTENTS

FOREWORD

There are certain people who, upon first meeting them, you recognize a special quality about them and you know that you will become fast friends. Patty Juster is such a person to me. Her intense love for Jesus, sensitivity to the Holy Spirit, and profound faith forged in the fires of testing, wrapped in humility, humor and grace makes her one of my favorite people.

Each of us will recognize *The Cry* within ourselves as we live the pages of this book. While Patty introduces *The Cry* as akin to that of a woman in the final throes of childbirth, *The Cry* of pain, anguish, longing and desperation—directed to our God—is genderless and common to all serious believers. Patty has experienced that cry in a number of situations and has discovered a spiritual principle. *A desperate people receive supernatural intervention.*

Because of the season and the signs of the times, members of the body of Christ need to be aware of, and giving themselves willingly to, how Jesus is equipping us *to rend the heavens, release grace, and prepare the way of the Lord.* This book is a heartfelt message to go deeper into yourpain to discover the depths of God's grace, love and faithfulness.

There is a redemptive purpose for everything you experience in life. God has created us to be co-laborers with Him to fulfill His plan for this earth. My prayer is that you will fall more deeply in love with Jesus as you discover the intense depths of His merciful love for you.

—Jane Hansen Hoyt
President/CEO of Aglow International

INTRODUCING *THE CRY*

"It's time to push!" may be the sweetest words heard by a woman about to give birth, for they declare the imminent end of hard labor. More importantly, these words herald the arrival of her child is at hand. After her nine-month wait, hope and its fulfillment begin to converge as the woman's body almost takes over. Every cell contracts to push the baby out. Nurses, doctors, and midwives begin to scurry around to get the instruments and themselves in place. Everyone focuses and strains to see the crowning of the head, a moment all have been anticipating. The mother has worked hard, and now just the mention of seeing the baby's head renews her strength. The final encouraging words are spoken—"You can do it! He is almost here!" And with this, she gives her final push. She expels, as it were, all of her life's breath so that now her little one emerges into being. But all through her process—all through her labor—the words spoken to her focused, directed, encouraged, and strengthened her. They delivered her in her delivery.

How we need such words today as the coming of our Lord nears. News of almost daily suicide bombings in Iraq, Israel, and other parts of the world are broadcasted from every media source. Because of modern technology, we are able to receive each day's account of the number of lives lost as the perpetrators of the crimes obtain instant, constant fame through extensive publicity.

A few years ago, there were several serious earthquakes. The one in Iran took over 30,000 lives. Then, there was the underwater quake in the Indian Ocean that generated the horrific tsunami, killing more than 150,000 people in mere minutes! Then, there was the devastation from Katrina in New Orleans. More recently there was a major earthquake in Haiti where tens of thousands died. And fumes from a volcano erupting in Iceland stopped European flights for almost two weeks. Shortly after this incident a major oil rig exploded in the Gulf of Mexico spewing out thousands of barrels of oil a day. It is said to be the worst oil spill in history. While this was going on Nashville was experiencing the worst flooding in the their whole recorded climatic history. In the midst of all this, I was reminded of Scripture:

> As Jesus was sitting on the Mount of Olives, the disciples came to him privately. "Tell us," they said, "when will this happen, and what will be the sign of your coming and of the end of the age?" Jesus answered: "Watch out that no one deceives you. For many will come in my name, claiming, 'I am the Christ,' and will deceive

many. You will hear of wars and rumors of wars, but see to it that you are not alarmed. Such things must happen, but the end is still to come. Nation will rise against nation, and kingdom against kingdom. There will be famines and earthquakes in various places. All these are the beginning of birth pains."

Matthew 24:3–8

As hard as it may be for us to believe, this Scripture says we're only in the early stage of labor.

Additionally, Romans 8 tells us that even creation's longings are manifested as the groans of a woman in labor. All of creation (and that includes us) is and has been groaning in anticipation of the fulfillment of all the promises of God's word since the beginning of time.

We know that the whole creation has been groaning as in the pains of childbirth right up to the present time. Not only so, but we ourselves, who have the firstfruits of the Spirit, groan inwardly as we wait eagerly for our adoption as sons, the redemption of our bodies.

Romans 8:22–23

Through the pains of childbirth all creation is groaning to be restored to what to what God initially intended, a place that is not subject to decay and corruption. It groans for a time where the wolf will lay down with the lamb and the lion will eat straw like the ox. And as violence intensifies amongst the people of the earth we too groan for a time where there will be no more sorrow or pain or death. All creation is intricately connected as what man does actually affects the created world around him. So all creation cries out for the redemption of mankind that we might come into our inheritance as sons of God.

Sin is a burden to all and its consequential suffering reminds us that our life here is temporal. It would only stand to reason then that, the closer we come to the return of the Lord, the more intensive and the more frequent the labor contractions. If the birth analogy holds up, there will be a time of "pushing," where the "mother" switches gears and no longer cares whether she lives or dies, since all that matters is getting the baby out. In the last days, we are told that the believers will come to the point of not loving our own lives "even unto death." I can imagine we will be gripped with passion for seeing the return of Lord and will see that somehow our courage and endurance in the midst of suffering will eventually rend the heavens and prepare the way. We long for this day, the redemption of our bodies at the resurrection where we will be refined and made gloriously beautiful, without corruption. We will be declared to be God's sons and our adoption will be complete for we will become like the One whom we behold. The joy of the coming of our Savior will be worth all the pain! But before the time of the "great push," there will be a time of great suffering. It is not the pains of one dying but of one giving birth to the new heaven and the new earth. Scripture refers to this critical stage as a call to patiently endure. (See Revelation 13:10; 14:11–12.) This is where in the natural the mother often loses it and cries out.

In the summer of 2003, I was privileged to attend my daughter at the birth of her first baby. For days, she experienced false labor and found herself on edge—tense with the expectation of the imminent birth of her baby. Though she felt the kicks of her child hourly in her womb, she could only develop a relationship of love and connectedness through touch and not sight. At times, her experience of carrying her child within her felt surreal. Anxiously, she anticipated the birth experience and often rehearsed everything she learned in her birthing classes. My daughter, Rebecca, opted to deliver in a birthing center run by midwives, as she wanted a perfectly natural birth. She wanted to feel all the pain involved in the labor process, so she could really appreciate the joy of seeing her precious little girl. Rebecca expressed her disapproval of the predominant philosophy of childbirth where doctors treat giving birth as a sickness, as something that has to be medicated or treated as a medical problem that needs hospitalization. Years ago, women gave birth at home, and pain was accepted as the price to be paid for the joy of the prize of motherhood. Sure, for some women hospitalization is necessary, but for her she wanted to go the natural route.

Finally, the day arrived, and the labor pains took on a serious dimension. Because of the hours of preliminary labor, it did not take long before she was ready to settle down to intense labor. As each labor contraction came and went, my daughter rode the waves of pain through groaning. I was taught the Lamaze method of childbirth, where one used a focal point to stare at while the contraction intensified. To manage the pain, I would use different kinds of breathing techniques. However, this groaning method that my daughter used was different, and it reminded me of the accounts in the Bible of the labor process where women groaned in the midst of their pain. I became increasingly aware of the Holy Spirit's highlighting the dynamics of this birthing process as if to tell me, "Take note!"

In between the moans and groans, I encouraged my daughter with words like, "You are doing so well, Rebecca. It won't take long now before you will be able to hold your little girl." I sat on the edge of the bed and held her right hand while her husband held her left.

As the labor became more intense and moved through transition, it became increasingly more difficult to maintain control. Instead of riding the pain, the pain was riding her, especially as the time came for her to push. At one point, she let out a desperate scream from deep within her. Some might call it blood-curdling. She did not cry out, "Mom," or "Dad," or "Chad" (her husband) but "Jeeessuss!" And then, she cried out that she could not go through with it. The midwife gently but firmly told her that she should not scream like that because it was taking oxygen away from the baby. The midwife encouraged her instead to push with all her strength for the sake of the baby. Then, I chimed in that I saw the baby's head.

A supernatural grace empowerment from God kicked in, and she switched gears. Rebecca tucked in her chin and puffed her chest out with a determination, proclaiming, "I can do this!" At that moment, she no longer feared the pain but rose above it and pushed with all her might. That one push just about ejected the baby from her cozy home. At once, everyone burst into tears of laughter and joy at the sight of the beautiful new baby girl, Layel

Samhe Holland. The joy that comes after the pain of labor is indescribable! Such jubilation erupted from our souls. Out of the depths of pain, a joy unspeakable broke forth from deep within our souls. Yes, all the pain was worth the prize of this precious little girl!

Jesus, we are told, bore the pain of the cross for the joy set before Him. Could this be another birthing analogy? I think so. Furthermore, we are told to follow in His steps to endure and even rejoice in our suffering because of what will be born. This book will hopefully encourage you and impart faith to release the cry of faith to birth the end-time purposes of the Lord and His eventual return. It is a prophetic intercessory cry that will corporately unite us when we with one voice and one cry call forth the coming of our Lord and Messiah. Without Jesus's coming to set up His Kingdom, we cannot go on. He is our only answer.

God is preparing His intercessors first by teaching them the cry of faith to release the grace of God in their own lives. Only then will they have the authority to use what they have learned for the sake of setting others free through releasing grace on the behalf of others. Individuals, families, congregations, cities, Israel, the nations, and eventually the world will be birthed into their inheritance as we do our part. Let us yield to each labor contraction as God moves us on to that great and glorious day. "Amen. Come, Lord Jesus" (Revelation 22:20).

LEARNING *THE* ℂRY

Early in the morning, after the birth of our granddaughter, I went home to sleep. Watching the miracle of birth never gets old, and each time I experience the wonder as new. When I awoke the next morning, I knew I had to listen to the birth experience I recorded on an audio tape seventeen years ago at the birth of our youngest child, Samuel Peter. Just like my daughter, I had reached a point in my labor where I could no longer bear the pain, and I let out "the scream." And of course, the midwife gave me a pep talk (I delivered my youngest at home), and I switched gears. Before long, I was pushing with abandonment, and I no longer feared tearing or hurting. What mattered was no longer how I felt but the life of the baby. That baby was coming out even if it killed me! Love strengthened my resolve.

Soon the head came out, then the arms, and then my husband received the baby into his arms and held up our precious little boy, Samuel Peter. We all burst into tears of joy and laughter. Love flooded our hearts in the communal drama. Every time I listen to this tape, I get caught up in that moment of extreme emotion. And enter into new joy and wonder mingled with tears. This time, however, when I listened to that tape it added sorrow to the joy as Samuel only lived twelve years. In June of 1998, Samuel Peter died from his injuries sustained in a house fire. New waves of grief descended on me as I relived his birth through listening to the tape. Memories of the lessons God taught me came to mind. He reminded me of the connection between the birth pangs of labor and the waves of the labor of grief. Right after his death, God revealed this truth to me and encouraged me from the book of John.

> Jesus saw that they wanted to ask him about this, so he said to them, "Are you asking one another what I meant when I said, 'In a little while you will see me no more, and then after a little while you will see me'? I tell you the truth, you will weep and mourn while the world rejoices. You will grieve, but your grief will turn to joy. A woman giving birth to a child has pain because her time has come; but when her baby is born she forgets the anguish because of her joy that a child is born into the world. So with you: Now is your time of grief, but I will see you again and you will rejoice, and no one will take away your joy."
>
> John 16:19–22

God told me then that if I would embrace the grief as labor pains, and yield to Him in the midst of the pain, He would birth more of Himself in me through revelation. And when I had come through this grieving process, He assured me that He would give me a joy that no one would be able to take away. I needed this assurance and soon found out that His word to me was true. As I yielded to each "labor contraction" of grief, He released grace. Some contractions lasted a few minutes, and some lasted longer. Often the length of the pressure of grief became longer when I resisted the pain. During these seasons, the grace seemed to lift, and I would go into depression. He taught me that my depression happened when I rebelled against the grieving process. In a way, I had to intently focus on Jesus in much the same way I had to focus on an object outside of myself during real labor. When my eyes were open again to the goodness of the Lord, I repented and returned to His loving embrace. I received in my spirit the all sufficiency of His grace, and the weight of grief lifted until the next season of labor.

I held on to the promises of the word where God promised to turn the sorrow and mourning of the Jewish people to joy and gladness, believing that one day He would do the same for me.

> … and the ransomed of the LORD will return. They will enter Zion with singing; everlasting joy will crown their heads. Gladness and joy will overtake them, and sorrow and sighing will flee away.
>
> Isaiah 35:10

The Spirit of the Sovereign LORD is on me, because the LORD has anointed me to preach good news to the poor. He has sent me to bind up the broken-hearted, to proclaim freedom for the captives and release from darkness for the prisoners, to proclaim the year of the LORD's favor and the day of vengeance of our God, to comfort all who mourn, and provide for those who grieve in Zion—*to bestow on them a crown of beauty instead of ashes, the oil of gladness instead of mourning, and a garment of praise instead of a spirit of despair.*

Isaiah 61:1–3, 9

Then maidens will dance and be glad, young men and old as well. I will turn their mourning into gladness; *I will give them comfort and joy instead of sorrow.*

Jeremiah 31:13

I also held onto the examples in Scripture concerning different men and women who cried out to God in the midst of their pain. It was their cries that moved the heart of God, and He acted in response to their tears.

Scriptures seem to indicate that our sorrow does have an effect on Him. Through the days, months, and years after Sam's death, I put this truth to the test again and again. On many occasions, I would abandon myself to releasing my intense pain through crying out to God. For many going through the grieving process, there is a fear that, if you give yourself to crying, you will not be able to stop. The enemy deceives us into believing that the pain is bottomless and that grieving will kill us. However, as long as I grieved with Godly grief, God lifted the tears at just the right time. When He was in control, the pain was not greater than I could bear.

I have so many glorious memories of crying out to God while I was alone in my car, my bedroom, the shower, or the woods. I poured out my heart to Him, and each time He was faithful to do an exchange of His strength for my weakness. Through adversity, I learned the power of *The Cry* for rending the heavens and releasing His grace. Bit by bit, God was teaching me and building faith in His ability to take care of my soul.

Most of us learn *The Cry* through personal crisis. This cry will go up to the only One who can save. It can happen in the midst of a life-threatening situation, or it can occur when the pain of injustice or when intense physical pain gets too great. Sometimes, we cry out when we are in a crisis and we need wisdom. Usually, we cry out when all other resources of relief or answers have dried up, and personal resources come up short.

Recently, I completed my first book, *Refined by Fire*. In it, I recounted suffering loss after loss and the treasures I gleaned during those dark periods. For example, just six months after my son died, my mother died of cancer. Then, some other dear friends died. Also, I experienced a season of serious heart malfunction, and I was facing surgery. Change came to our home as our two oldest children were married. And then, we went through a terrible, heart-rending "divorce" as we experienced the loss of our home congregation we had shepherded for twenty-two years. As the result of unwise decisions that were made during the period of transition of leadership, we were cut off from our precious flock. With each new loss or change, the scabs of healing over the wound of the loss of our son were painfully ripped off, as it were, and each new pain was contaminated and magnified. This led to more gut-wrenching crying out.

I remember one particular occasion when I believe I cried out my loudest and longest cry. It was the day after the birth of my daughter's baby. The couple who took over our congregation happened to be our daughter's in-laws, and the morning after the birth of our granddaughter, I decided to go see my daughter and her prize. When I arrived, her in-laws were already there holding the baby.

Something snapped inside me as my daughter sent me on an errand when I wanted to be the one staying behind to hold my precious granddaughter. I was driving along in the car on the errand when I became overwhelmed with grief and sorrow. An intense feeling of injustice gripped me, and my internal pain thermometer burst. This event seemed to trip the switch of my accumulated pain—not merely the pain over the present situation but over all the situations. It was more than I could bear, and I let out a continued, toe-curling scream from the depths of my being. My cry went forth as a trumpet, heralding the heavenly hosts to come to my rescue. It was deep, as if my insides were turning inside out, and it felt almost like I was being repeatedly stabbed by an assailant. It sounded similar to a birthing scream, and I called out the name of Jesus at the top of my lungs!" It was just like my daughter did the day before. He alone could save me. Every cell of my body knew that there was no hope unless God came through, and as I cried out, I lifted up my soul to the source of all resurrection life. Then, the One called Faithful and

True showed up and did His exchange thing. He turned my mourning into joy as I released *The Cry*. How He does this thing, I cannot tell you. All I know is that He is the only answer sufficient to alleviate the depth of the pain and suffering in this world. Only God can calm the storm of raging injustice.

I burst into tears of joy, as I understood why I had to go through all this loss and sorrow. He showed me that He was putting inside me a treasure, the assurance of Jesus being the only One adequate to heal the tremendous pain in the heart of the Jew. God was preparing me for Israel and the body of believers; giving me a message of the all-sufficient power of Jesus. He truly bears our pain and lifts us from the miry pit.

We may not receive justice in this life, but we have a Comforter who will keep us sheltered beneath His wings until the time for the avenging of our blood comes. We can endure because *Jesus endured injustice*, yet He knew no sin. We have a king who reigns from a throne where the Lamb sits, One who has been slain from before the foundation of the world (Revelation 13:8). Because of this, we can have confidence in a Savior who can sympathize with our pain and sorrow. He alone has the power to lift it from us at the right time.

We are no longer victims but children of a loving Father, who is working in us such a glorious salvation. All His ways are just and true. He is the One who created the destroyer to wreak havoc, and He is the One who has somehow bound us all into a story of His writing. It is a living story of the dynamics of God's sovereignty, our choices, and the evil forces seeking to destroy us. Somehow, God brings us through to believe in Him whom we do not see, to believe that He is always good. He gives us the grace to love and to trust in Him. It is such a mystery how God reveals His great love in the face of such suffering and moves us to love Him in return.

One day the veil will be removed, and we will see God in all His brilliant wisdom and magnify His glorious character and deeds. We will see that all His actions are just and true (Revelation 15:3–4). Worship will erupt from our souls, uniting us with the great cloud of witnesses in heaven. Through God's dealings with us, we transfer our citizenship from here to the eternal kingdom of heaven, invisible yet more real as the days pass. He purges us of worldly attachments so that what remains is the love of the Father.

> Do not love the world or anything in the world. If anyone loves the world, the love of the Father is not in him. For everything in the world—the cravings of sinful man, the lust of his eyes and the boastings of what he has and does—comes not from the Father but from the world. The world and its desires pass away, but the man who does the will of God lives forever.
>
> 1 John 2:15–17

Surely, He brings us to the place where we live and move and have our being in Him!

I am called to intercede for others so that this revelation is birthed in them. As the Apostle Paul wrote of his travail that Messiah would be formed in those whom he loved, so I, too, am called to birth God's purposes in the lives of people. *Through my suffering, God gave me revelation and understanding of the kind of intercession that would one day rend the heavens and release the eventual return of the Messiah. It was through crisis that I learned The Cry.* It is an intercession that has grown out of a heart of compassion forged in the furnace of much affliction.

THE CRY TO RELEASE PERSONAL GRACE

Our frantic seeking for relief in the midst of pain often leads us to put wrong expectations (weight) on the arm of the flesh to save us. And then, when men (especially authorities in our lives) fail to relieve our pain or to protect us, we often turn on them. As long as there is a human being around we can blame for our mistakes, losses, or injustices, we will not turn to God wholeheartedly. We will never wrestle with God through the dark hours if we do not believe in God's sovereignty over us. Yes, men do sin against us, but ultimately we have to face God as the One who has allowed all the circumstances in our lives. At any time, He could choose to deliver or prevent, yet for reasons we do not quite understand, sometimes He allows something bad to befall us. In fact, the Scriptures below evidence God even may cause it.

> Blessed is the man whom God corrects; so do not despise the discipline of the Almighty. For *he wounds, but he also binds up; he injures, but his hands also heal.*
> Job 5:17–18

> Come, let us return to the Lord. *He has torn us to pieces but he will heal us; he has injured us but he will bind up our wounds.* After two days he will revive us; on the third day he will restore us, that we may live in his presence. Let us acknowledge the Lord; let us press on to acknowledge him. As surely as the sun rises, he will appear; he will come to us like the winter rains, like the spring rains that water the earth."
> Hosea 6:1–3

> I will be his father, and he will be my son. *When he does wrong, I will punish him with the rod of men, with floggings inflicted by men.*
> 2 Samuel 7:14

> Who can speak and have it happen if the Lord has not decreed it? *Is it not from the mouth of the Most High that both calamities and good things come?*
> Lamentations 3:37–38

We must push through the cloud of obscurity to see God as the source of blessing, even though He simultaneously may be the source of temporary pain. He is good and can be trusted even in the midst of pain and confusion. Light will break forth as we receive this revelation. He chastens the one whom He loves. Can we come to the place of faith to believe there is no contradiction between the concept of a good and loving God and the concept that sometimes God inflicts wounds that we might be healed?

In the course of our everyday lives, we may find ourselves in the midst of sudden impending danger. With no time to philosophize or debate about the doctrine of God's sovereignty, *The Cry* flies in the face of this looming threat. It only takes a second to yell, "J-e-e-e-s-s-s-u-u-u-s-s-s," and often God responds even if *The Cry* is uttered from the lips of unbelievers. He honors the use of the name that is above all names. But, if there is any possibility that our own prowess can save us, this is what we will try first.

Some of us are slow to learn our own finiteness or powerlessness and, therefore, do not believe that God will respond to our cry for help in the midst of personal crisis. *We unconsciously base our lack of trust in God's faithfulness on our own past experiences with authorities in our lives.* We, consequently, see God through the colored glasses of our experiences with broken promises, verbal and physical abuse, and betrayal and disappointment. Although we may believe that God will usually deliver us from life-threatening situations (for we are acutely aware of our powerlessness in these situations), we still may find it hard to believe that God will release grace for us to endure in the form of renewed strength or in the form of relief in the midst of emotional pain or adverse circumstances.

How *The Cry* is Released

Let me go into a little more detail concerning the dynamics of what is going on before the release of *The Cry*. Before *The Cry* is released, we must learn that God is sovereign and recognize that nothing He purposes in His heart will be thwarted. His arm is never too short in that He can choose at any time to save.

Before this "cry of faith" is released, we must have received personal revelation of who God is and of how He truly wants to work all things together for our good. And that type of revelation only comes through repeated failures of lesser fixes. Yet, no matter how deeply we believe this, sometimes we fall back to our default setting and choose other methods of relief or deliverance such as overeating, sexual perversion, alcohol, or too many video games. Then, as if some light goes on in our heads again, we come to our senses and realize once again that God is our only hope. *We are broken by the moment of powerlessness and are overcome by our awareness of great weakness in the face of the present adversity. We look at the impending danger or at the magnitude of our pain and know beyond all shadow of doubt we are no match. What a glorious place to be when we are made weak. For then the door is opened for us to receive a strength that is not our own!*

The magnitude of the revelation of the glorious riches of God's grace comes into focus deep within our spirit in the face of great weakness. How could we ever know the depths of His grace if there was never a need to draw upon it? The Apostle Paul realized this and was able to write of his joy in the midst of severe hardships.

But he said to me, "My grace is sufficient for you, for my power is made perfect in weakness." Therefore I will boast all the more gladly about my weaknesses, so that Christ's power may rest on me. That is why, for Christ's sake, I delight in weaknesses, in insults, in hardships, in persecutions, in difficulties. For when I am weak, then I am strong.

2 Corinthians 12:9–10

It is at that breaking point where we acknowledge our inability that *The Cry* is released. It feels as though something has left us, and on the way out, it feels like our very being has been torn in two. I believe that it is at this point that we lose our lives and God does His exchange thing by replacing our lives with His. (We are "crucified with the Messiah, and it is no longer we who live but the Messiah who lives in us.") *In response to our cries, He rends the heavens, and delivers us, or the people for whom we are standing in the gap.*

Not all crying out can be categorized under the term, *The Cry*, as we often give up or cry out of self-pity, anger, or frustration. (However, sometimes, God will act out of His great mercy in response to such cries.) "The cry of faith" cannot be self-induced. Just as the timing of labor pains are under the control of God's sovereignty, so too is the release of this cry. It is not a formula or a method to get God to act on our behalf. Rather, *The Cry* is a response to our desperate situations. It is a turning to God instead of man for our healing or deliverance. When God brings to the point of birth, He is faithful to deliver. He has heard and will hear our cries.

The Effect of Trauma

At certain junctures in life, one can become traumatized by the shock of loss, danger, accident, or abuse. Trauma affects our ability to trust and to cope with future hurts. Yet, God is faithful; He wants us to be well in body, soul, and spirit. He does not grow weary as He leads us into greater and greater wholeness. God wants us to live in the reality of our sonship, no longer doubting His love and goodness. Our trust, organs, and our hearts, have been battered, and God heals us through more wounding, as strange as this may seem.

I see God as being a homeopathic healer in that whatever causes our wound to begin with is what He used to fix us. For example, if we were wounded by rejection, it seems we keep on getting rejected or imagine we are being rejected. This happens so that we may learn to overcome this adversity in the power of His grace. We come to see that we are not victims of another's rejection; in other words, we do not have to take it personally. We have a choice of how to respond. We do not have to reject the person in return but can keep on loving him or her. And, most of time, the other person really isn't rejecting us; we are just projecting rejection on them.

It is easy to trust when everything is going well. But, when bad things happen, we are tempted to doubt. However, through God's faithfulness to us in the midst of various trials, we can come to fully trust Him again and be released into the glorious freedom as sons of God. *Adversity reveals our weaknesses and His strength. We come to know Him in greater and greater intimacy and come to understand our dependence on His grace for every breath. We become sons through suffering.*

Of course, not everyone has these deep traumatic experiences of lost loved ones, betrayal, rape, or abuse that warrant such a cry, and not all have been in a life-threatening condition. You may have never needed to voice such a cry. Still you can glean truths from this book that might be useful in days ahead, or you may be able to encourage others with this message. He is able to save us to the utmost! Psalm 23 must be a living reality for each of us in the days ahead. God is in the business of restoring souls. Our souls find rest in Him alone, and when we come to truly believe this, we will have the courage to yield our soul into God's hands in every crisis.

Ripping and Tearing

As stated before, *The Cry* happens when we realize that we are powerless to change the course of what has happened to us in the past or to prevent harm from a present impending danger. How can one bring back from the dead the life of a loved one, or get back virginity, or procure his or her own rescue when overpowered by greater forces? Therefore, *The Cry* often comes with a ripping and tearing as when a woman gives birth. We are told that Jesus let out a deep cry when He died on the cross, and the veil of the temple was torn in two.

> *And when Jesus had cried out again in a loud voice, he gave up his spirit. At that moment the curtain of the temple was torn in two from top to bottom.* The earth shook and the rocks split. The tombs broke open

and the bodies of many holy people who had died were raised to life.

Matthew 27:50–54

What power was in His cry! It was a cry of faith to the only One who could save. It was the release of His soul into the hands of His loving Father. A way was made for us to enter into intimate fellowship with God through this act. We are told in Hebrews that we can come boldly to the throne of God because Jesus made a way through His flesh that is called the veil. A veil separated the holy of holies from the Holy Place. This veil, His body, was torn and bloodied for our freedom. "Therefore, brothers, since we have confidence to enter the Most Holy Place by the blood of Jesus, *by a new and living way opened for us through the curtain, that is, his body*" (Hebrews 10:19–20).

Could it possibly be that at the point where we release our "cry," giving up our hold on self-protection, that the curtain of our hearts is rent and a way is open for greater intimacy with God? Perhaps there are veils that hide or block us from seeing Jesus as He really is, and these veils need to be torn in two. I believe this to be true, and God is preparing us to release through corporate intercession with the united prayer of both Jew and Gentile. Such a cry will rend the heavens, removing the veils over the hearts of the lost, and finally *The Cry* will open a door for the return of Jesus. Isn't it interesting to note the Jewish tradition of tearing one's garment when one has lost a close loved one? Also, examples are given in the word of prophets tearing their garment as an act of horror or grief in the face of great sin. Was this a symbolic foreshadowing of the temple curtain tearing in two, and now can it be seen as a prophetic intercessory act? Veils are torn so that there might be sight!

Conclusion

The Lord is our Shepherd, and we have no lack or deprivation. He is the Supplier of our soul's food, and we no longer have to manage our own lives or the lives of others in an attempt to protect ourselves from pain. How grateful I am to God for He is preparing me for the difficult days ahead, and has taught me how to abide under the shadow of His wings. He is releasing faith for yielding to *The Cry* not just to relieve my own pain but also to cry over the pain of others and intercede for their deliverance. Also, I know that this tool of intercession will be used in the face of impending judgment where corporately those who have come to this place of freedom can cry out in faith to the merciful God to spare His people or to repent on behalf of a people group as did Ezra, Nehemiah, or Daniel. "Lord, we have sinned and deserve death, but you are a merciful and gracious God who loves righteousness and justice. In wrath, remember mercy!"

Perhaps you are one of those God is preparing as a type of Esther (whether you're a man or woman) to stand before the king and to cry out for the lives of others. Maybe you have gone through seasons of bitterness and blame shifting as you have found yourself in an emotional prison. Hope seems buried, as nothing appears sufficient to handle all the accumulated pain. You cannot even imagine what there could be to make your life worth all the painful trials you have been through. Paul stated that his light and momentary troubles could not be compared to the glory that would be his. This may not compute in our minds. How can a man who had been stoned, whipped, and shipwrecked come to this conclusion? There must be something so great in his revelation of Jesus that daily empowered him to continue the race of preaching the good news of the gospel of grace. And what did Moses see (Hebrews 11:24–27) that gave him courage to suffer with his people and to confront the mighty Pharaoh?

I believe that you will receive sight as you patiently embrace your suffering, turning from all pointing of the finger at others. As you run into the arms of your Savior and pour out your heart to Him, the veil will be ripped in two. Then, you will see Jesus in greater glory. It is only in His presence that you will receive comfort and understanding. He is faithful. And will come through for you as He has for millions before you.

These conclusions have come through life experiences in conjunction with confirmation of the word. As I have poured over God's encouragement in the Scripture, His Spirit illumined verses that gave me hope. The principle of *The Cry* has its basis in the Bible. Time and time again, we can perceive through Scripture how God is truly attentive to the cries of His people. As a mother's heart is moved with compassion when she hears her baby cry and seeks to comfort her child, so too God's heart is moved. Come with me as I take you on a journey through the revelation of the Holy Spirit and the Word.

THE CRY HEARD

God imparts faith through (1) the Word, (2) our personal experience, or (3) the testimony of others. Usually, faith comes in conjunction with these three operating together. I know that Scriptures such as the ones below gave me courage to hold onto the promises of God's deliverance in the midst of prolonged adversity.

> Some wandered in desert wastelands, finding no way to a city where they could settle. They were hungry and thirsty, and their lives ebbed away. *Then they cried out to the* LORD *in their trouble, and he delivered them from their distress.* He led them by a straight way to a city where they could settle. Let them give thanks to the LORD for his unfailing love and his wonderful deeds for men, for he satisfies the thirsty and fills the hungry with good things.
>
> Psalm 107:4–9

The LORD said, "I have indeed seen the misery of my people in Egypt. *I have heard them crying out because of their slave drivers, and I am concerned about their suffering.* So I have come down to rescue them from the hand of the Egyptians and to bring them up out of that land into a good and spacious land, a land flowing with milk and honey."

Exodus 3:7–9

The cords of the grave coiled around me; the snares of death confronted me. In my distress I called to the LORD; I cried to my God for help. From his temple he heard my voice; my cry came before him, into his ears. The earth trembled and quaked, and the foundations of the mountains shook; they trembled because he was angry. Smoke rose from his nostrils; consuming fire came from his mouth, burning coals blazed out of it. He parted the heavens and came down; dark clouds were under his feet … He reached down from on high and took hold of me; he drew me out of deep waters. He rescued me from my powerful enemy, from my foes, who were too strong for me.

Psalm 18:5–17

The righteous cry out, and the LORD *hears them*; he delivers them from all their troubles.

Psalm 34:17

Evening, morning and noon *I cry out in distress, and he hears my voice.* He ransoms me unharmed from the battle waged against me, even though many oppose me.

Psalm 55:17–18

For he will deliver the needy who cry out, the afflicted who have no one to help. He will take pity on the weak and the needy and save the needy from death.

Psalm 72:12–13

But he took note of their distress when he heard their cry; for their sake he remembered his covenant and out of his great love he relented.

Psalm 106:44–45

I waited patiently for the LORD*; he turned to me and heard my cry.* He lifted me out of the slimy pit, out of the mud and mire; he set my feet on a rock and gave me a firm place to stand. He put a new song in my mouth, a hymn of praise to our God. Many will see and fear and put their trust in the LORD.

Psalm 40:1–3

As these Scriptures indicate God sustains us through our adversity, and He also delivers us from it. But during our very devastatingly personal adversity, our responses to suffering can either harden our hearts or bring us into the inner courts of the Most High. The truth will set us free because God's word is sharper than any two-edged sword. It is precise and powerful to the dividing of soul and spirit.

In the midst of great suffering, the enemy of our soul, Satan, tempts us to even accuse God of wrongdoing. We question God's goodness as it feels as if even He has failed us. How can a good and loving God allow such pain and suffering? Because of the increase of evil, as the word says, many hearts will grow cold. Even though judgments are poured out upon mankind, and mankind knows the judgments are from the hand of God, there are some who will still refuse to repent (Revelation 18:8–11). *Yet, dear reader, be assured that God hears our cries, and they move Him to act.*

Waiting

Sometimes, it feels like we do not even have faith as we grow weary of waiting for God to act. You may be in a season of prolonged suffering, and it may seem as though the heavens are as brass. Hours have turned into days, days into weeks, weeks into months, and sometimes months become years. "How long, Lord?" may be your perpetual cry. There are many verses in the book of Psalms that express the agony of the soul in the midst of apparent silence. *When our tears seem to go unheard, it is a season where our cry will deepen, and our faith will be strengthened.* Trust me. I know what I'm talking about. The Lord will bring to remembrance His faithfulness and unfailing love of the times He came through for us in the past.

> But I cry to you for help, O Lord; in the morning my prayer comes before you. Why, O Lord, do you reject me and hide your face from me?
>
> Psalm 88:13–14

> O my God, I cry out by day, but you do not answer, by night, and am not silent. Yet you are enthroned as the Holy One; you are the praise of Israel. In you our fathers put their trust; they trusted and you delivered them. They cried to you and were saved; in you they trusted and were not disappointed.
>
> Psalm 22:2–5

I cry out to you, O God, but you do not answer; I stand up, but you merely look at me.

Job 30:20

O Lord, the God who saves me, day and night I cry out before you. May my prayer come before you; turn your ear to my cry. For my soul is full of trouble and my life draws near the grave. I am counted among those who go down to the pit; I am like a man without strength.

Psalm 88:1–4

Hear my prayer, O Lord; let my cry for help come to you. Do not hide your face from me when I am in distress. Turn your ear to me; when I call, answer me quickly...But you, O Lord, sit enthroned forever; your renown endures through all generations. You will arise and have compassion on Zion, for it is time to show favor to her; the appointed time has come...For the Lord will rebuild Zion and appear in his glory. He will respond to the prayer of the destitute; he will not despise their plea. Let this be written for a future generation, that a people not yet created may praise the Lord...

Psalm 102:1–2, 12–13, 17–180

Though the answer tarries, we are encouraged to wait for His deliverance. *Those who put their hope in God and wait for Him instead of taking matters into their own hands will be strengthened. Through patience and faith, we will inherit the promises.*

God Hears the Cries of His Servants

Hannah is an example of a person who cried out in bitterness of soul because of her barrenness. Having a barren
womb often is the occasion for much grief. We cry out
sometimes when a blessing is denied or delayed. Many
times, our tears will move God to answer our hearts' desires.
We are all familiar with the story of Hannah. And, how
God granted her the desire of her heart. Out of gratitude
to God and in response to her promise, she gave Samuel
over to the Lord to serve him all the days of his life.

> In bitterness of soul Hannah wept much and prayed
> to the LORD. And she made a vow, saying, "O LORD
> Almighty, if you will only look upon your servant's
> misery and remember me, and not forget your ser-
> vant but give her a son, then I will give him to the
> LORD for all the days of his life, and no razor will
> ever be used on his head." As she kept on praying
> to the LORD, Eli observed her mouth... "Do not
> take your servant for a wicked woman; I have been
> praying here out of my great anguish and grief." Eli
> answered, "Go in peace, and may the God of Israel
> grant you what you have asked of him."
>
> 1 Samuel 1:10–12

> I prayed for this child, and the LORD has granted me
> what I asked of him. So now I give him to the LORD.
> For his whole life he will be given over to the LORD.
> And he worshiped the LORD there.
>
> 1 Samuel 1:27–28

God birthed a prophet after His own heart out of Hannah's heart of great anguish. Perhaps you are wondering why God hasn't answered your heart's desire for a baby or a husband or a wife or a ministry or something else. We live in a fallen world, and sometimes the promises in Scripture are given as corporate blessings for an obedient people. Our western mindset interprets much of Scripture individualistically; therefore, we miss the prerequisites for the blessings listed in Exodus or Deuteronomy. These promises were conditional. If Israel, not if individuals like Moses or Aaron or Joshua, would obey God's law, then these blessings would follow the entire nation. There would be no one who miscarried, there would be no one who was barren among them, and they would be "the head and not the tail."

Nowhere in the world are all of these blessings operating at this level in a community of people. Some individuals may be able to walk in these blessings, but if we have not attained to them, we are not to come under condemnation. These promises are true whether or not we see their fulfillment in this life as they are awaiting a time to be evident in the midst of an obedient people.

Another example of God's hearing the cries of His servant is the story of Jehoshaphat. He was one who found favor with God through his obedience in bringing reform to Judah. In the day of battle, when his enemies rose up against him, he gathered an assembly of those who feared God. Together they entered a season of fasting and crying out to God. God heard their prayers and delivered them. In Jehoshaphat's despair, he cried out to God for wisdom, as he did not know what to do. In response, God gave him assurance of His deliverance and gave him a battle plan. God hears our cry for wisdom.

> Then Jehoshaphat stood up in the assembly of Judah and Jerusalem at the temple of the LORD in the front of the new courtyard and said: "O LORD, God of our fathers, are you not the God who is in heaven? You rule over all the kingdoms of the nations. Power and might are in your hand, and no one can withstand you. O our God, did you not drive out the inhabitants of this land before your people Israel and give it forever to the descendants of Abraham your friend? They have lived in it and have built in it a sanctuary for your Name, saying, 'If calamity comes upon us, whether the sword of judgment, or plague or famine, we will stand in your presence before this temple that bears your Name and will cry out to you in our distress, and you will hear us and save us' … See how they are repaying us by coming to drive us out of the possession you gave us as an inheritance. O our God, will you not judge them? For we have no power to face this vast army that is attacking us. We do not know what to do, but our eyes are upon you." All the men of Judah, with their wives and children and little ones, stood there before the LORD … "You will not have to fight this battle. Take up your positions; stand firm and see the deliverance the LORD will give you, O Judah and Jerusalem. Do not be afraid; do not be discouraged. Go out to face them tomorrow, and the LORD will be with you." Jehoshaphat bowed with his face to the ground, and all the people of Judah and Jerusalem fell down in worship before the LORD.
>
> 2 Chronicles 20:5–9, 11–13, 17–18

May we gain new hope to cry out for wisdom as Jehoshaphat did when we find ourselves in situations where there seems to be no answer. Scripture admonishes us that crying out for wisdom is the way to release this grace.

> … and if you call out for insight and cry aloud for understanding, and if you look for it as for silver and search for it as for hidden treasure, then you will understand the fear of the Lord and find the knowledge of God.
>
> Proverbs 2:3–5

A third example of someone in the Bible crying out to God and getting results was Hezekiah. God added fifteen years to his life when Hezekiah cried out to Him in the midst of his sickness and delivered him from the king of Assyria.

> Remember, O Lord, how I have walked before you faithfully and with wholehearted devotion and have done what is good in your eyes. And Hezekiah wept bitterly. Then the word of the Lord came to Isaiah: "Go and tell Hezekiah, 'This is what the Lord, the God of your father David, says: I have heard your prayer and seen your tears; I will add fifteen years to your life. And I will deliver you and this city from the hand of the king of Assyria. I will defend this city.'"
>
> Isaiah 38:3–6

God Is Merciful to the Unsaved

God is so merciful that He even responds to the cries of those who are not of the faith of Abraham. He is moved by the tears of the sons of Isaac as well as the sons of Ishmael! I believe that the cries of those who are enslaved by the Islamic spirit have risen to God, and He is about to act like He did for Ishmael so many years ago. Additionally, I believe the tears of abused women and children especially affect the heart of God.

> Early the next morning Abraham took some food and a skin of water and gave them to Hagar. He set them on her shoulders and then sent her off with the boy. She went on her way and wandered in the desert of Beersheba. When the water in the skin was gone, she put the boy under one of the bushes. Then she went off and sat down nearby, about a bowshot away, for she thought, I cannot watch the boy die. And as she sat there nearby, she began to sob. God heard the boy crying, and the angel of God called to Hagar from heaven and said to her, "What is the matter, Hagar? Do not be afraid; God has heard the boy crying as he lies there. Lift the boy up and take him by the hand, for I will make him into a great nation." Then God opened her eyes and she saw a well of water. So she went and filled the skin with water and gave the boy a drink.
>
> Genesis 21:14–19

God's Mercy Embraced

Our weakness in the face of adversity influences God's decisions when we look to Him for strength. In Deuteronomy 8, we are told that God brought the Israelites through the desert to test them in order for them to see what was in their hearts. He humbled them, causing them to hunger after Him and not just after food. "For man does not live by bread alone but by every word that proceeds from the mouth of the Father." *How would we ever get to the point of deep understanding of who we are apart from adversity? And this knowledge comes more by knowing who Jesus is in us when we have been made weak.* It is said of Abraham that against all hope in hope he believed. His faith was strengthened as each year went by while he was waiting for the fulfillment of the promise of a son. I pray that your faith will be strengthened as you gain encouragement from the testimony of Scripture. *God hears our cries! We can come boldly before His throne and obtain mercy and grace in time of need. And then, when we have been comforted with the comfort that comes from God, and have been strengthened through God's grace, we can in turn comfort and strengthen others.* We will be a vessel fit for noble purposes. God can then trust us to intercede for His mercy to be released towards others.

THE CRY TO RELEASE MERCY FOR OTHERS

God is faithful to hear our cries! And we all can receive the personal grace released when we cry out to Him. But sometimes, when our souls (mind, will, and emotions) are weak within us and we draw near to death, we come to the point of despair where we cannot cry out for ourselves. At times like these, He raises up those who will stand in the gap for us.

Life can be so cruel that our only means of coping is to shut down. I have been there! God's grace is sufficient even for this serious condition. *God will stir the hearts of His servants to intercede and those who obey will stand before Him and cry out for those who are initially in despair and cannot or refuse to turn to Him.* How desperately God is looking for those who will stand in the gap as He is not willing that any should perish. He knows we are but dust. *As He finds those who yield to Him in the midst of their trials, He can train them to cry out for mercy towards others. He has chosen to use us in redeeming the world not because He is unable to save others without us, but because He in His wisdom and great love decided to make us co-laborers with Him.*

When we have come face to face with our own pain and have dealt with the injustices in our own lives, then God often uses us to cry out for the needs of others. (He uses us even before we are fully mature.) God will call upon us to stand in the gap when others are not in the place of faith to cry out because of their unbelief and the hardening of their hearts. *There is one kind of power when we cry out for ourselves and an even greater power when we cry out for others.* Just think of Abraham who had such favor with God that God heard his plea for Sodom and Gomorrah. God was willing not to destroy these cities if He found even ten righteous people living there.

Moses cried out for the Israelites when God was about ready to wipe them all out and make him a father of many nations in place of Abraham's seed. God heard the prayer of Moses and released the grace of forgiveness to His people Israel time and time again.

We can thank God for His prophets. They, too, often cried out for mercy towards the people of Israel: "They said to Samuel, *'Do not stop crying out to the* LORD *our God for us,* that he may rescue us from the hand of the Philistines'" (1 Samuel 7:8).

The priests of Israel were admonished to stand in the gap on behalf of the people, and sometimes God came through by relenting of the calamity He had planned.

"Even now," declares the Lord, "return to me with all your heart, with fasting and weeping and mourning." Rend your heart and not your garments. Return to the Lord your God, for he is gracious and compassionate, slow to anger and abounding in love, and he relents from sending calamity. Who knows? He may turn and have pity and leave behind a blessing—grain offerings and drink offerings for the Lord your God. Blow the trumpet in Zion, declare a holy fast, call a sacred assembly. Gather the people, consecrate the assembly; bring together the elders, gather the children, those nursing at the breast. Let the bridegroom leave his room and the bride her chamber. Let the priests, who minister before the Lord, weep between the temple porch and the altar. Let them say, "Spare your people, O Lord. Do not make your inheritance an object of scorn, a byword among the nations. Why should they say among the peoples, 'Where is their God?' Then the Lord will be jealous for his land and take pity on his people."

Joel 2:12–18

When they had stripped the land clean, I cried out, "Sovereign Lord, forgive! How can Jacob survive? He is so small!" So the Lord relented. "This will not happen," the Lord said.

Amos 7:2–3

Even our youngest daughter, Simcha, has experienced a call from God to cry out on behalf of her friends. One time, she cried out for the salvation of her friends with such intensity that others thought someone was murdering her. It happened one Friday evening before our Shabbat dinner at the home where we were spending the summer in Israel. She was having some time alone with the Lord, trying to catch up on her fellowship with God through worship and reading the word. I had gone back to her room to check on her, and she began to explain the revelation she was receiving from the Lord concerning His heart for His people as recorded in the early chapters of the book of Ezekiel. Then, this intense grief for the lost came upon her, and she began to scream out at the top of her lungs and wailed for the hearts of her friends in the army. (She was serving in the Israeli army). She abandoned herself to *The Cry* for mercy while the guests in the other room were horrified. Thankfully, they were all believers, so when I came out of our daughter's room and explained what was going on, they all breathed a sigh of relief. They strongly admonished us to give them some warning next time—to let them know before we released this level of intercession!

These tears that we shed for others are a God-given gift. It does no good to try to work them up. It is God who gives us such a heart of compassion where we weep for another. One time, I was ministering to a woman who was in bondage to smoking. I sensed that she suffered great shame for her failure to quit, and I knew that she had been injured many times by well-meaning Christians. I did not want to heap more condemnation on her. God began to break my heart for her, and I started to weep for her and ask God for His mercy and grace to come through. It was only after I softened the way through tears that I felt liberty to speak to her. To make a long story short, she was set free, went off cigarettes cold turkey, and has not had another cigarette for months. It was God's compassion that set her free!

God, stir us up to care about the hurting and the lost—those who are too hardened to cry out for themselves. No greater love can we have for others than to lay down our lives for them. Spending time interceding is costly; it is sacrificial. Oh, to have eyes to see the impact our prayers make on the unseen world. *Praying rends the heavens and releases righteousness and salvation on the earth.* "You heavens above, rain down righteousness; let the clouds shower it down. Let the earth open wide, let salvation spring up, let righteousness grow with it; I, the LORD, have created it…" (Isaiah 45:8).

The Apostle Paul cared so much for others coming to salvation that he said he was willing that he himself be cut off from the presence of God for the sake of his brothers after the flesh. This is true intercession! He cared nothing about the comforts of this life, and he was compelled to preach the good news of the gospel of grace until the day he died. His great love for Jesus constrained him; therefore, he had grace to offer his life as a living offering unto God's purposes.

Such praying releases grace for spiritual growth for others. The Apostle Paul cried out on behalf of the believers that the Messiah would be formed in them. He kept them continually in his prayers that they may know the depth of God's love for them and that the eyes of their hearts would be enlightened. He wanted others to know the perfect will of God and come to the fullness of the knowledge of God. Paul often compared his intercession to travail as a woman in labor. How his heart burned within to see God's kingdom manifest on earth in every realm.

Perhaps Paul was willing to endure such adversity for the sake of the gospel because of his gratitude for God's forgiveness and forbearance towards him. Because he experienced such liberty and joy in his salvation, he longed that others shared in this glory. He was so caught up in the purposes of God that he often spoke of his spiritual children as his crown and joy!

Paul took up ownership with God and was to share in His suffering in order to receive his inheritance along with Jesus. His inheritance was the people of the world—the same inheritance spoken as a promise to Abraham. God promised Abraham that he would be an heir of the world. When we have this mindset, we are more willing to fight for what is ours. Employees that share in the profit of a company are often more willing to give one hundred percent effort in their job than those who view themselves as just a hired hand.

> The hired hand is not the shepherd who owns the sheep. So when he sees the wolf coming, he abandons the sheep and runs away. Then the wolf attacks the flock and scatters it. The man runs away because he is a hired hand and cares nothing for the sheep.
>
> John 10:12–13

This principle of joint ownership is so important. We must see that we are shareholders in the kingdom of God. Without participating in this concept, we will not give one hundred percent in establishing God's kingdom on earth. We will not pay the price to bring others fully into the purposes of God. We will have an attitude that says, "Let God do it. The people belong to Him. If He wants them, He can save them. He doesn't really need me." And then, when the going gets tough, we will readily give up and run away from our calling. It is much easier to let someone else lay down His life. What we do not understand is that if we stop fighting for life, life in ourselves and life in others, we will die. God has set up our existence here on earth as being corporate in nature. We are not islands unto ourselves.

The body of Christ works much like the human body in that when a part gets infected, fighter cells from other parts of the body come to the aid of the cells surrounding the wounded area. Together they fight off their common enemy—death. If the body ceases to fight for the life of the body, then it dies. When we stop being concerned for another's welfare, we will die, for love has ceased. The word says that we know when we pass from death to life when we love one another. Anyone who does not love remains in death. And when we love, we are willing to lose our lives for the sake of others.

We see that we are fighting for a corporate expression of the life of God manifested on earth as a living testimony. If Satan can seduce us into passivity, then he has won the battle. The testimony of the life of God would be defamed, and death would triumph. Then, it would be proven that God did not have the power to bring us into our promised land, and He really didn't defeat the power of death. The keys of hell and death would still be in the hands of the evil one, but they are not; the keys are in the hands of this corporate expression.

As soon as we enter the world, forces of evil are arrayed against us to rob, steal, and destroy. If Satan is not permitted to snuff out our physical lives, then he works to harden our hearts—in other words, to kill us spiritually. Whenever we are sinned against, the power of death is enlarged against us. Bitterness, anger, un-forgiveness, rejection, violence, envy, hatred, etc., all spring up within (if we do not go to the cross for power to overcome), and we in turn become instruments of releasing death towards others instead of life! Whenever evil befalls us through tragedy and other events, death stares us in the face of our spirits. If we cower in fear, the doors of our hearts shut down to the life of God, and we participate in a process of distancing ourselves from our Source. We must overcome these forces of evil through the spiritual weapons of warfare assigned us through the Holy Spirit. Intercession is one of the most powerful weapons of our warfare.

The Apostle Paul made an appeal to his fellow believers to continue praying fervently for him for his deliverance. He recognized his dependence on the body to come to his aid in prayer to fight off the attacks of the enemy.

> We do not want you to be uninformed brothers, about the hardships we suffered in the province of Asia. We were under great pressure, far beyond our ability to endure, so that we despaired even of life. Indeed, in our hearts we felt the sentence of death. But this happened that we might not rely on ourselves but on God, who raises the dead. He has delivered us from such a deadly peril, and he will deliver us. On him we have set our hope that he will continue to deliver us, as you help us by your prayers.
> 2 Corinthians 1:8–11

Prayer

Oh Lord, we confess that we have allowed our own hearts to become desensitized to the needs of others. We have not valued Your gift of life to us. Open our eyes so we can understand our role in releasing Your life in this world. Help us to see the worth of our inheritance and take up ownership as co-heirs with You, being willing to suffer as You suffered for the sake of Your honor. We confess that our eyes have been blinded to this pearl of great price. We want this revelation.

Resurrect us from the dead so we have the motivation to fight for others and to cry out for their resurrection. Give us Your heart of love for others so we will be willing to lay down our lives, if this is what it would take, for others to come to the fullness of Life in You. We recognize that this prayer can only be answered by You, for in no way can we love like this in our own strength.

Open our eyes to Your plumb line of righteousness (God's standard of righteousness found in His son) and expose areas in our own lives that are not pleasing to You so we will not be self-righteous in our prayers for others. Enable us to be tender toward those in sin without condoning their lifestyles. Break through, oh God, for the sake of the honor of Your holy name! Amen.

THE CRY TO RELEASE MERCY BEFORE JUDGMENT

Scripture not only depicts *The Cry* that releases mercy for others, but the word also portrays occasions when *The Cry* is released so that mercy is pronounced in order to stay God's hand of judgment. Here are just some of such appeals:

> When the news reached the king of Nineveh, he rose from his throne, took off his royal robes, covered himself with sackcloth and sat down in the dust. Then he issued a proclamation in Nineveh: By the decree of the king and his nobles: "Do not let any man or beast, herd or flock, taste anything; do not let them eat or drink. But let man and beast be covered with sackcloth. Let everyone call urgently on God. Let

them give up their evil ways and their violence. Who knows? God may yet relent and with compassion turn from his fierce anger so that we will not perish." When God saw what they did and how they turned from their evil ways, he had compassion and did not bring upon them the destruction he had threatened.

Jonah 3:6–10

"They have taken some of their daughters as wives for themselves and their sons, and have mingled the holy race with the peoples around them. And the leaders and officials have led the way in this unfaith-fulness." When I heard this, I tore my tunic and cloak, pulled hair from my head and beard and sat down appalled. Then everyone who trembled at the words of the God of Israel gathered around me be-cause of this unfaithfulness of the exiles. And I sat there appalled until the evening sacrifice.

Ezra 9:2–4

While Ezra was praying and confessing, weep-ing and throwing himself down before the house of God, a large crowd of Israelites—men, women and children—gathered around him. They too wept bitterly.

Ezra 10:1

Oh, my anguish, my anguish! I writhe in pain. Oh, the agony of my heart! My heart pounds within me, I cannot keep silent. For I have heard the sound of the trumpet; I have heard the battle cry. Disaster follows disaster; the whole land lies in ruins. In an instant my tents are destroyed, my shelter in a moment. How long must I see the battle standard and hear the sound of the trumpet?

Jeremiah 4:19–21

"See, I will send venomous snakes among you, vipers that cannot be charmed, and they will bite you," declares the LORD. O my Comforter in sorrow, my heart is faint within me. Listen to the cry of my people from a land far away: "Is the LORD not in Zion? Is her King no longer there? Why have they provoked me to anger with their images, with their worthless foreign idols? The harvest is past, the summer has ended, and we are not saved." Since my people are crushed, I am crushed; I mourn, and horror grips me. Is there no balm in Gilead? Is there no physician there? Why then is there no healing for the wound of my people?

Jeremiah 8:17–22

These cries or appeals were intense in the face of judgment—so intense that such cries were compared repeatedly to the pain of a woman in labor. Can you imagine agony so great that one writhes or pants and trembles? Such was the pain experienced by these prophets who heard the sound of the trumpet releasing God's judgment. They cared so much for the people they served that news of impending judgment undid them. It is hard for us to relate to this kind of intensity as the Western church has become so compromised with the world. Because of the increase of wickedness, the hearts of many have grown cold, and they can't even respond. The language used to describe the pain of these prophets seems so foreign. How can their agony be compared to a woman giving birth? Isn't this a little extreme? But maybe their hearts were deeply impacted with God's heart for His people? Maybe they saw that their intercession would "birth" mercy for his people? Thank God, they saw that He did not want to carry out the fierce wrath His holiness demanded. He preferred mercy over judgment and wanted so much for men to come to repentance so He would not have to cause so much devastation and suffering.

> I hear a cry as of a woman in labor, a groan as of one bearing her first child—the cry of the Daughter of Zion gasping for breath, stretching out her hands and saying, Alas! I am fainting; my life is given over to murderers.
>
> Jeremiah 4:31

> Writhe in agony, O Daughter of Zion, like a woman in labor, for now you must leave the city to camp in the open field. You will go to Babylon; there you will be rescued. There the LORD will redeem you out of the hand of your enemies.
>
> Micah 4:10

> As a woman with child and about to give birth writhes and cries out in her pain, so were we in your presence, O LORD. We were with child, we writhed in pain, but we gave birth to wind. We have not brought salvation to the earth; we have not given birth to people of the world.
>
> Isaiah 26:17–18

> Terror will seize them, pain and anguish will grip them; they will writhe like a woman in labor. They will look aghast at each other, their faces aflame.
>
> Isaiah 13:8

At this my body is racked with pain, pangs seize me, like those of a woman in labor; I am staggered by what I hear, I am bewildered by what I see. My heart falters, fear makes me tremble; the twilight I longed for has become a horror to me. They set the tables, they spread the rugs, they eat, they drink! Get up, you officers, oil the shields! This is what the Lord says to me: "Go, post a lookout and have him report what he sees."

Isaiah 21:3–6

For a long time I have kept silent, I have been quiet and held myself back. But now, like a woman in childbirth, I cry out, I gasp and pant. I will lay waste the mountains and hills and dry up all their vegetation; I will turn rivers into islands and dry up the pools.

Isaiah 42:14–15

When the kings joined forces, when they advanced together, they saw [her] and were astounded; they fled in terror. Trembling seized them there, pain like that of a woman in labor.

Psalm 48:4–6

These men were talking about the heart essence of *The Cry* where all human hope seemed lost and against all hope they turned to the God of hope who was sovereign over all. He was the One who could do whatever He purposed in His heart to do and was the only One who could raise up a man into kingship and the only One who could bring down the pride of the arrogant. *Somehow, their faithfulness in yielding to The Cry either limited the devastation or the extent of God's wrath, or it averted it altogether.* History has proven the power of effective prayer.

They abandoned themselves to the purposes of God in releasing a lament.

Oh, the travail of the soul that is released through suffering or identification with those who suffer; God is pleased with those who cry out on the behalf of others or mourn over the sins of a people in identification. So much so, He once told an angel to mark the foreheads of those who mourned and lamented over their sins and the sins of their city. Those people whose foreheads were marked were spared in time of judgment.

> Now the glory of the God of Israel went up from above the cherubim, where it had been, and moved to the threshold of the temple. Then the LORD called to the man clothed in linen who had the writing kit at his side and said to him, "Go throughout the city of Jerusalem and put a mark on the foreheads of those who grieve and lament over all the detestable things that are done in it." As I listened, he said to the others, "Follow him through the city and kill, without showing pity or compassion. Slaughter old men, young men, and maidens, women and children, but do not touch anyone who has the mark. Begin at my sanctuary." So they began with the elders who were in front of the temple.
>
> Ezekiel 9:3–6

We have become so desensitized to sin in the world that it is hard to find those whose hearts are smitten at the mention of wrongdoing. We have seen so much violence and immorality, or heard so much cursing on TV that when we actually experience these things on the streets we usually are not shocked. When Josiah read the Book of the Law while he was a king, his heart was smitten. He was convicted about the sin in Judah and understood that the things she was doing was setting her up for judgment. In horror, he tore his robe and cried out to God. Nehemiah, Ezra, and Daniel also wept when their eyes were opened to the condition of their people. Their prayers affected history! But today, if what others are doing doesn't directly affect our comfort, we think, "Why rock their boat?" Where is the outrage against the new trend that is sweeping our country? Where is the church to speak out against the gay marriages and the increasing ungodliness of our nation?

On the opposite side, there is the issue of a judgmental heart. It is so easy to pronounce judgment on others, dismissing them from our hearts in self-righteousness. Many of us can recognize sin in others, but instead of interceding for them in humility, we easily erect walls of judgment that separate us. We often speak about these people to others in a detached sort of way. Probably what we are seeing is true, but *where is the heart that weeps and grieves over what it sees? Where are those who will stand in the gap to be an advocate instead of a prosecutor?* There is a time for speaking the truth, but only after we see the person from God's perspective and heart. We must love the one in sin so much that we are willing to confront as we see that their sin is hindering them from coming into their destiny in God. It is for the good of the other that we speak up, not because of fear or irritation or some abuse we might have received from them.

And then, when we hear of impending judgment against those who are in sin, perhaps a friend who betrayed us, or a city or a nation that has turned its back on God, do we have an attitude of gratitude because God is finally going to give it to them? Or do we enter into intercession as a Daniel or a Nehemiah and pray, "Lord, we have sinned, we and our forefathers. Please forgive us as our sins are grieving your heart"? In humility, we recognize our own sinfulness and comprehend that all have sinned and come short of the glory of God. We all deserve judgment as God has bound us all over to disobedience that He might have mercy on us all. How we all should hit our knees and plead to God for mercy for those we know are certainly on their way to judgment. We need to align our hearts with God's heart. He desires mercy before judgment and will make grace available for repentance if we but lay hold of His intention through our intercession.

Each person, each city, or nation has a redemptive purpose in God. Sin hinders us from receiving our inheritance. Sin blocks the glory of God from shining forth in our life, and eventually, sin reaps judgment when left un-repented. God desires that His glory fill the earth, and He will not grow weary until He has established His righteousness. *Let's stand in the gap for mercy to stay judgment.*

THE CRY OF CHOSENNESS

Two weeks ago, my husband and I returned from a four-month stay in Israel. While we were living there, we experienced the aftereffects of several suicide bombings. Reading a newspaper in Israel about these events is certainly different from reading about them in the United States. And we won't even go into the vast differences of news reporting found in Europe and the Arab countries. Suffice it to say that experiencing news firsthand truly changes your perspective. Because of my own tragedy, I was supersensitive to the sufferings of the Jewish soul. Because of the fresh events of terrorism, the tough Jewish veneer broke apart, and I perceived *The Cry* deep within their DNA.

I realized while I was in Israel that the Jewish people are daily on the news, and God's dealing in their lives is broadcasted all over the world. The consequences of their sin are magnified not just through the recounting of their history in the Scripture but from well-meaning pulpit preachers and misinformed media moguls. Who can bear such a burden of being made a public spectacle in each generation? The shame barometer must be off the chart!

One can only imagine the generational stigma of shame that the Jews carry as God's chosen people. If they are chosen, why does God allow them to be so mistreated? Talk about a need for inner healing! Everywhere they go, each nation may eventually kick them out, accusing them of being the cause of everything that is wrong in the said nation. If the country is in economic crisis, then it is the Jews' fault. If there are not enough jobs to go around, then it is the Jews' fault. They appear to play the role of the scapegoat wherever they go. And then, when they are finally in their own land, the surrounding nations conspire against them to remove them from it. They never seem able to set up a permanent dwelling place and they are still living in "tents," as it were. Hence, the stigma of being a perpetual wandering Jew remains.

Throughout history, those who call themselves *Christians* have been known to blame the Jews for crucifying their Lord. Yet in Jesus's own words, we are told that no man had the power to take His life unless it was given to him from above. In Isaiah 53:10, we read that it was the Lord's will to crush Him and cause Him to suffer. Acts 4:27–28 highlights this: "Indeed, Herod and Pontius Pilate met together with the Gentiles and the people of Israel in this city to conspire against your holy servant Jesus, whom you anointed. They did what your power and will had decided beforehand should happen."

Revelation 13:8 further enlightens us when it says that Jesus was the Lamb "slain from the foundation of the world." When it comes right down to it, *God gave His only Son* for the atonement of our sins, and *Jesus willingly laid down His life*, submitting to the will of His Father. So the blame that has been placed on the Jewish people for everything from a nation's poor economic conditions to the crucifixion of Jesus has increased their sense of shame in being wrongfully accused.

When Dan and I were in Israel the summer of 2003, I was staying in Jerusalem with some friends while he was on a prayer journey in Africa. Late one night during this visit, Israel had a suicide bombing a few minutes away from the house where I was staying. I could hear the bomb blast and the sound of numerous sirens that seemed to blare for hours. The next morning, I felt compelled to go to the site of devastation and pray. When I arrived, there was a British TV crew interviewing different Israelis about whether they thought the president's Roadmap to Peace would work and whether or not this bombing would cause the person being interviewed to want to leave Israel. One man, when asked this question, responded with, "Where else can we go? There is no safe place for us. What choice do we have? We cannot let this threaten us and cause us to flee." Indeed, where can they find freedom from their enemies? And, why is this so?

In Judaism the word chosenness reflects the belief that the Jews are a chosen people who have entered into a covenant with God. According to Deuteronomy 14:2 God chose the Israelites to be his treasured people from all the nations. With their history of persecution, pogroms, holocaust, and numerous other sufferings, some among the Jewish race say, "Chosenness, who needs it?" The very term "chosenness" has provoked many to jealousy towards the Jews in much the same way as Cain was jealous of Abel and Joseph's brothers were of him. "Who has the Father's favor?" Mankind seems to ask. We all watch and notice carefully who appears to get the bigger piece of the pie, or who appears to receive other symbols of being the favorite child. We equate chosenness with being chosen first when sides are picked for baseball, or chosen for the starring role in a play, or perhaps chosen to be president of a company. *When someone else is chosen, we interpret this to mean that we were not chosen because there was something wrong with us.*

Perhaps we are inferior in some way, we think. *Not being chosen threatens our position and identity with the one who has done the choosing.* We often churn inside and reason that the chooser chose the wrong person or people. Jealousy grows, and if not stopped, it will eventually seek to destroy the ones chosen. I believe the heart behind the theology of replacement, where the church has replaced Israel as being chosen, arises out of an inability to accept Israel as God's chosen people. Jealousy is a cruel taskmaster, and without being aware of its motivation, jealousy can become a driving force behind much destructive behavior (James 3:16).

We can see the forces of evil throughout history, and even today, to obliterate all distinctions. It is as if man cannot stand the thought of there being differences between him and another. Women, even, seem put out that men are different from them, so they strive to be equal in every regard. The poor want there to be equality in possessions. The races want there to be no distinctions. Relativists do not want any absolutes, so there can be no value of one religion over another…all are equal and no person or choice is to be preferred over another.

I am aware that I am perhaps oversimplifying these issues, but I've become aware that there is an increasing tyranny to make everyone the same. In this way, mankind believes that war will be done away with as everyone will stand equally, thus ridding the world of jealousy and strife. Sounds good, doesn't it? But this will never happen as God has created variety. He has created a world where relationships of mutual blessing exist; that is, each created thing is unique, and as it relates to other created things, God ordained for them all to be mutually beneficial, not necessarily equal. He did this to release His grace in all its various forms. If we were all the same, then it would be very boring. I would have no need of you, and you would have no need of me.

One only has to look at God's creation to see all the variety of flora and fauna. What quality of life would there be if all the flowers were daisies and all the animals were German shepherds? Differences are for the purpose of releasing mutual blessings. And even the difference between male and female and between Jew and Gentile, though there are no distinctions in relationship to the Lord, exists for the purpose of mutual blessings.

Since Adam, each generation became progressively
worse until God eventually had to destroy mankind and
beast alike and start over again with Noah and his family.
But alas, it was not too long before man became united
in evil again and attempted to build a name for himself in
building the Tower of Babel (Genesis 11:3–7). God then
had to scatter the people throughout the earth, confus-
ing their language. "Then they said, 'Come, let us build
ourselves a city, with a tower that reaches to the heavens,
so that we may make a name for ourselves and not be
scattered over the face of the whole earth'" (Genesis 11:4).

God knew that by speaking one language they would
join forces to perform greater and greater acts of evil. He
did not want to destroy mankind again, so He looked for
a faithful man through whom He could build a covenant
people whose hearts would be loyal. He wanted a people
who would be the righteous remnant of mankind to preserve the human race. This nation would show forth the
wisdom of God by living out the requirements of His
holy law. Others would see the favor (blessings) of God
upon this people and come to the knowledge of Him.

God found such a man in Abram and made him to
be the father of faith to all who would believe. Abram
would be the seed from which a nation would be birthed.
Through his descendants, God would impart blessings to future generations that would eventuate in the
nations acknowledging the one true God. Therefore,
God's understanding of chosenness is quite different
when seen from the perspective of releasing blessings.
God chose Abram because He found a man who was

willing to listen and obey and to convey the will of God to his children.

> Abraham will surely become a great and powerful nation, and all nations on earth will be blessed through him. For I have chosen him, so that he will direct his children and his household after him to keep the way of the LORD by doing what is right and just, so that the LORD will bring about for Abraham what he has promised him.
>
> Genesis 18:18–19

His chosenness was not for the purpose of prestige or power but for the purpose of blessing the nations (Genesis 12:2–3). *Salvation was to come to the nations of the world through the Jewish people.* Neither Adam nor Noah nor any other man of faith before Abram was successful in teaching the law of God to the next generation. (It is interesting to note the anomaly of there always being a faithful remnant since the time of Abraham who has been zealous to maintain the life of Torah in their lives. No other people group has been so resilient to assimilate into the cultures where they might have been transplanted.) This people would be the nation that would stand in the gap and be the righteous remnant that would preserve the human race. And through this people came the human ancestry of the Messiah, who would ultimately bring salvation to all who believe—"to the Jew first and also to the Gentile."

Abraham's priestly role, which provided the spiritual DNA for future generations, can be seen in two major events. The first event was Abraham's response to the news from the angels that God intended to destroy

Sodom and Gomorrah. He stood in the gap and pled with God to spare these two cities for the sake of fifty, forty, thirty, twenty, or even ten righteous people. Of course, only Lot and his family were spared as not even ten righteous people could be found. Because of Abraham's faithfulness, he had influence with God, and God heard his cry for mercy.

The second important occasion that revealed the priestly call of this ancient people was when Abraham obeyed God and was willing to sacrifice his only son, Isaac, the child of promise, on the altar. Thankfully, God was just testing Abraham's faith and provided a ram to be the sacrifice before Abraham actually plunged the knife into his son. Through this act of obedience, Abraham offered back to God the human race and became a type of high priest for all mankind. Thus, this act released God to send His only Son to be the sacrifice to purchase back mankind from the enemy of his soul forever. For two thousand years, sacrifices were performed by the priests of Israel which participated somehow in the merit of Abraham's sacrifice. These sacrifices were efficacious for the preserving of a remnant people as well as the preserving of the nations of the world. In God's mercy, He provided this means by which He would not have to totally destroy the human race again.

God was not in a hurry, so He took years to form this earthly people. As part of the "education" of this chosen race, Abraham was warned by God that his descendants would be enslaved and mistreated for four hundred years. Some reward for being chosen?!

Then the LORD said to him, "Know for certain that your descendants will be strangers in a country not their own, and they will be enslaved and mistreated four hundred years. But I will punish the nation they serve as slaves, and afterward they will come out with great possessions. You, however, will go to your fathers in peace and be buried at a good old age. In the fourth generation your descendants will come back here, for the sin of the Amorites has not yet reached its full measure."

Genesis 15:13–16

The time in Egypt was compared to being in an iron smelting furnace, so it was said that God chose Israel out of the furnace of much affliction (Deuteronomy 4:20). *This affliction was not because of something Israel did that was bad, but because of their chosenness to represent the people of the world as a firstfruits offering to God* (more will be said about firstfruits later), *insuring a harvest among the peoples of the world.* Four hundred years was a long time to be enslaved, though we are not sure from Scripture exactly how long it was after Joseph and his brothers died that a Pharaoh began to get threatened by the increase in numbers of the Israelites.

"Look," he said to his people, "the Israelites have become much too numerous for us. Come, we must deal shrewdly with them" ... So they put slave masters over them to oppress them with forced labor, and they built Pithom and Rameses as store cities for Pharaoh. But the more they were oppressed, the more they multiplied and spread; so the Egyptians came to dread the Israelites and worked them ruthlessly. They made their lives bitter with hard labor in brick and mortar and with all kinds of work in the fields.

Exodus 1:9–14

Through the years of intense suffering, a cry was birthed deep within the soul of the Israelites. They began to groan in their slavery "and cried out, and their cry for help because of their slavery went up to God. God heard their groaning and he remembered his covenant with Abraham, with Isaac and with Jacob. So God looked on the Israelites and was concerned about them" (Exodus 2:23–25). For this reason, God raised up a deliverer, Moses, and spoke to him from inside a burning bush.

> The LORD said, "I have indeed seen the misery of my people in Egypt. I have heard them crying out because of their slave drivers, and I am concerned about their suffering. So I have come down to rescue them from the hand of the Egyptians and to bring them up out of that land into a good and spacious land, a land flowing with milk and honey."
>
> Exodus 3:7–8

The land of Israel was a major part of God's covenant promises to this chosen race. Much of Israel's history is centered on obtaining this homeland and keeping it. Two conditions for their deliverance from slavery in Egypt had to be fulfilled in order for them to take up the ownership of Canaan. The first condition was that their cries rising from intense suffering come to fullness, and the second condition was that the wickedness of the Canaanites had to become full. (Genesis 15:16 explains, "For the sin of the Amorites has not yet reached its full measure.")

It is interesting to note this truth in the story of Sodom and Gomorrah. The evil in these cities became so great that an outcry rose against them. "The outcry against Sodom and Gomorrah is so great and their sin so grievous that I will go down and see if what they have done is so bad as the outcry that has reached me" (Genesis 18:20–21).

At the right time, in the fullness of time, God brought His people out of bondage through many great acts of deliverance. The death of all the firstborn of Egypt became the price that eventually purchased their freedom. Freedom is costly, and forever the value of even this sacrifice coming from a pagan nation, though it was not a voluntary sacrifice, is remembered through the priestly order within Israel.

Then, God shaped these people through His dealings with them, shaping them through hardships and trials in the wilderness. He wanted a people that would fully trust Him in all circumstances. He tried to train them to look to Him for their very sustenance. Time and time again, they failed the tests due to grumbling and rebelling against Moses and Aaron. Many times, they threatened to return to Egypt, feeling more secure in depending on their slave master for food.

A couple of weeks were not sufficient to teach them to trust God, so when they came to the place of entering into the promised land, they chickened out. They feared the giants and refused to trust God for their lives. Therefore, they had a more extended stay in the wilder-

ness—forty years! And all those adults who were enslaved
to their unbelief died in the desert over a period of forty
years. *Still, God's purposes for this people would prevail, and
He patiently disciplined the new generation to hear and obey
His voice. They learned that even the privilege of possessing
and maintaining the land of Israel was dependent on their
faith and obedience.* "Be careful to follow every command
I am giving you today, so that you may live and increase
and may enter and possess the land that the LORD promised on oath to your forefathers" (Deuteronomy 8:1). He
humbled them so that in the end it might go well with
them. He worked in their lives so that they would not get
into pride thinking it was through their skill or strength
that they obtained the land and produced wealth. He
taught them that man does not live by bread alone but
on every word that comes from the mouth of the Lord.

God repeatedly warned Moses that Israel's chosenness and the privilege of possessing the land of promise
was not because of her own righteousness but because of
the wickedness of the nations. He reminded Moses and
the people three times that their own integrity or righteousness was not the reason for their chosenness but
that the reason was found in the very purposes of God.
(See Deuteronomy 9:4–6.) In fact, God stated that their
character was the very opposite—that they were actually
a stiff-necked people.

God receives the glory when he chooses the weak and
the foolish to confound the strong and the wise! God's
plan from the beginning was that no one may be able to
say that it was their own wisdom or strength that accom-
plished God's purposes. Hence, in Israel, being chosen

for God's purposes entails a constancy of weakness and foolishness. Often, He put them through a long period of testing, trials, and suffering in order to bring them to a place of brokenness and obedience. Though Abraham was given the promise of being the father of many nations, and was given a promise of a son from Sarah who was barren, he waited twenty years for the fulfillment. And, even then, he did not see the complete fulfillment that would only be received by his future generations.

Most of us are familiar with the stories of Jacob, Joseph, Moses, and David. All bear the marks of chosenness in the midst of trials and afflictions to bring them to the place where God can really use them. As was true of certain key players in Israel's history, so is true of Israel as a nation. *As a nation, they bear the marks of being chosen in the midst of great suffering, and out of this weakness is birthed a cry, along with the added cry of the chosen from among the nations (Gentiles), sufficient to rend the heavens in the last days to release the return of the Lord.*

There are yet purposes of God for this chosenness that require a people to be made humble like Moses. Moses had a sense when he was a young man that he was called to deliver his people from bondage, but when he tried to procure their deliverance through his own strength, he dramatically failed. When he saw a fellow slave being mistreated by the slave master, he struck the man dead and then had to flee for his life as word spread about his deed. For forty years, he hid in the desert and attended sheep. As God humbled him during this time, he was purged of all ambition. At eighty years of age, God finally released him into his role as deliverer of his people, for which Moses severely resisted. Moses was so broken that even when God was angry with the six million Israelites and wanted to destroy them, Moses would fall on his face and cry out for mercy. If he were not a broken man, he would have allowed God to start over with him and build a faithful nation through his own descendants. Can you see the implications of this?

There is coming a time when God's wrath will be poured out upon the nations. It will be a time where Israel will have to stand in the gap for the nations. The word says that in the last days, after all the nations rise up and come against Israel, God will destroy by plague the nations that came against Israel:

> I will gather all the nations to Jerusalem to fight against it; the city will be captured, the houses ransacked, and the women raped. Half of the city will go into exile, but the rest of the people will not be taken from the city. The LORD will go out and fight against those nations, as he fights in the day of battle…This is the plague with which the LORD will strike all the nations that fought against Jerusalem: Their flesh will rot while they are standing on their feet, their eyes will rot in their sockets, and their tongues will rot in their mouths. On that day, men will be stricken by the LORD with great panic. Each man will seize the hand of another, and they will attack each other…Then the survivors from all the nations that have attacked Jerusalem will go up year after year to worship the King, the LORD Almighty, and to celebrate the Feast of Tabernacles.
>
> Zechariah 14:2–16

I want to note here that there are a significant growing number of righteous Gentiles in the midst of the attacking nations who will lay down their lives for the sake of Jesus's brethren after the flesh. God is already pouring through them unprecedented love for His people. This love is turning more and more hearts of Jewish people to reconsider Jesus.

If Israel were not a broken people and were still claiming victim status, they would feel self-righteous and be jubilant that God was punishing the people of the world. Yes, evil has to be punished, and the word says that there is a type of joy we have when justice prevails, yet even in judgment we cry out to God to remember mercy. Verse 16 refers to the survivors of the nations who came against Israel. They will come up to Jerusalem to worship the King. *Perhaps the prayers of this priestly people will determine how extensive the destruction will be and how many survivors there will be.*

Chosen to be a Firstfruits Offering

For some reason, in God's wisdom, He chose a people to demonstrate His dealings with mankind, "to the Jew first and also to the Gentile." As part of their chosenness, the Israelites are referred to as a kind of firstfruits, a people belonging to God.

> I remember the devotion of your youth, how as a bride you loved me and followed me through the desert, through a land not sown. Israel was holy to the Lord, the firstfruits of his harvest; all who de-

voured her were held guilty, and disaster overtook them, declares the LORD.

Jeremiah 2:2–3

When the firstfruit offering is made holy, it assures that the rest of the batch will be holy. *"If the part of the dough offered as firstfruits is holy, then the whole batch is holy;* if the root is holy, so are the branches" (Romans 11:16).

In Jewish tradition, a woman making the Friday night special Sabbath bread, Challah, would break off a piece of dough and burn it in the oven as a burnt offering. This was a way of expressing gratefulness for God's provision and the release of blessing on the rest of the work of her hands. *As God has refined His people as silver, He has established a holy people as a similar firstfruit offering to release blessing on the rest of the peoples of the earth.* In Malachi, we are told that judgment will come first to His priests and then to the rest of His people so that He will once again have a priesthood that will offer sacrifices in righteousness.

When you understand the principle of firstfruits, you will understand the cost to have this title. The firstfruits of the earth became an offering belonging to the Lord, and part of it was offered as a burnt sacrifice to the Lord to assure that the rest of the crop would be holy and acceptable. Leviticus 23:9–14 goes over the details of this sacrifice celebrated during the Feast of Firstfruits that took place during Passover.

Also, the firstfruits of the livestock, menservants, flocks, and herds were given to the priests. God inaugurated this principle because of the death of all the firstborn of the Egyptians, a price that was paid for the Israelite's freedom from slavery.

> On that same night I will pass through Egypt and strike down every firstborn—both men and animals—and I will bring judgment on all the gods of Egypt. I am the LORD.
>
> Exodus 12:12

> The LORD said to Moses, "Consecrate to me every firstborn male. The first offspring of every womb among the Israelites belongs to me, whether man or animal."
>
> Exodus 13:1–2

> "I have taken the Levites from among the Israelites in place of the first male offspring of every Israelite woman. The Levites are mine, for all the firstborn are mine. When I struck down all the firstborn in Egypt, I set apart for myself every firstborn in Israel, whether man or animal. They are to be mine. I am the LORD."
>
> Numbers 3:12–13

The whole nation was chosen to be priests, but during the testing at Mt. Sinai, they opted for Moses and Aaron to be their representatives before God. They feared they would die if God would speak to them like He spoke to Moses. So God established the tribe of Levi as a special priesthood. The tribe of Levi was chosen to be set apart as they were the only tribe to rally behind Moses and Aaron after the worship of the golden calf. When Moses said, "Whoever is for the LORD, come to me." All the Levites came to his side and then they were instructed to execute judgment. He commanded them to kill their brother and friend and neighbor, and about three thousand of the people died. (See Exodus 32:26–28.) "You have been set apart to the LORD today, for you were against your own sons and brothers, and he has blessed you this day" (Exodus 32:29). *So chosenness here is not just hearing the call but actually heeding the call.* Perhaps this is the meaning of the verse, "For many are invited, but few are chosen" (Matthew 22:14). Chosenness involves responding to the call.

Eventually, God set apart the Levitical tribe as a people belonging to Him in a special way. God became their inheritance, and they gave themselves fully to serving the Lord and the people. They were the buffer people between God and man. In fact, their tribe pitched their tents around the Tabernacle to prevent the wrath of God from breaking out against the rest of the Israelites.

> The Levites, however, are to set up their tents around the tabernacle of the Testimony so that wrath will not fall on the Israelite community. The Levites are to be responsible for the care of the tabernacle of the Testimony.
>
> Numbers 1:53

The Levites were there to cover the people through their temple service of worship and sacrifice. They taught the law to the people, settled disputes, and handled their sacrifices. They represented God to the people and brought the concerns of the people to God.

Within the Levitical priesthood, God prescribed an order in which the different duties of the tabernacle were divided. The closer a person was to touching the most holy articles or to ministering in the holy of holies, the more the demands of holiness upon his life. *With chosenness came greater responsibility and greater consequences for sin.* Moses was forbidden to enter the promised land as the result of one act of dishonoring God in front of the Israelites. Two of Aaron's sons were struck dead when flames from the presence of the Lord leapt from the holy fire and consumed them. They were killed because they did not honor God as holy when they offered unauthorized fire before the Lord. Only the High Priest was given this privilege and then only once a year on the Day of Atonement.

So we see that there are concentric circles of chosenness. Israel as a nation was considered a firstfruits offering among the nations belonging to the Lord. Then, the firstborn among the Israelites, both from among men and among beasts, especially belonged to the Lord. Next, we read of how the Levites were chosen in place of all the firstborn of Israel and were set apart for service to the Lord. Then, among the priesthood of Levites, the Koathites were set apart as the only ones who could touch the holy articles of the tabernacle. And among the Koathites, only the firstborn, Nadab, son of Aaron, was chosen to be the high priest who could go into the Holy of Holies once a year. However, since Nadab and Abihu died as a result of their sin, the privilege of high priest went to Eleazar.

> They were responsible for the care of the ark, the table, the lampstand, the altars, the articles of the sanctuary used in ministering, the curtain, and ev-

erything related to their use. The chief leader of the Levites was Eleazar son of Aaron, the priest. He was appointed over those who were responsible for the care of the sanctuary.

Numbers 3:31–32

It was the priests who performed the sacrifices brought to them by the Israelites for their sins. But only the high priest could perform the sacrifices on the Day of Atonement for his own sins as well as the sins of the community. And this could only be performed once a year where he would take a censer full of burning coals from the altar, incense, and the blood from the sacrifices behind the veil to perform his priestly duties.

Within the ranks of this chosen nation, there was jealousy over the order of priesthood. Moses and Aaron were opposed by Korah, Dathan, and Abiram. They accused Moses and Aaron of setting themselves up above the Lord's assembly and did not accept their status as being chosen by God to fulfill a particular function. As a result of this opposition, plagues or tragedy came upon the people who rose up in arrogance. (See Numbers 16:1–35.) According to Numbers 16:7, *"The man the* LORD *chooses will be the one who is holy."* The Lord demonstrated His choice of Moses and Aaron by causing the earth to open up and swallow up those who showed contempt for the Lord's chosen vessels.

In addition, fire came out from the Lord and consumed 250 men who were offering incense. Then, the Israelite community, as a whole, grumbled against Moses and Aaron, and God judged those who rebelled against the priestly order. A plague broke out among the people and killed 14,700 before

Aaron had a chance to stop the destruction through offering incense, and thereby making atonement for them. This was the occasion where God finally put an end to the grumbling against His chosen instruments by causing Aaron's staff to blossom, the only staff which blossomed (representing the tribe of Levi) among the twelve staffs representing the twelve tribes of Israel.

At that point, God gave a mandate to the priests. "The LORD said to Aaron, *'You, your sons and your father's family are to bear the responsibility for the offenses against the sanctuary, and you and your sons alone are to bear the responsibility for the offenses against the priesthood'*" (Numbers 18:1). In addition to being the sin bearers until the time of Jesus, they were called upon to give up any claims of inheritance among the Israelites. Instead, they were to be given the tithes that the Israelites presented as an offering to the LORD. God alone was to be their share and inheritance among the people of Israel. (See Numbers 18:20, 23.)

Jesus—Chosen and Firstfruits

Until the time of Jesus, the Levites continued to fulfill their role as sin bearers among the Israelites. But once Jesus died on the cross and rose again, He became "for all time [the] one sacrifice for sins" (Hebrews 10:12). Indeed, the writer of Hebrews clearly says, "We have been made holy through the sacrifice of the body of Jesus Christ once for all" (Hebrews 10:10). He, then, became our sin bearer, our scapegoat.

Like the Levites, the Israelites, Aaron, Moses, and Abraham, Jesus was chosen. Speaking of the Messiah, Isaiah 42:1 reads, "Here is my servant, whom I uphold, my chosen one in whom I delight; I will put my Spirit on him and he will bring justice to the nations." *And because Jesus was God's Chosen One, He suffered the ultimate agony of His chosenness—death upon the cross.* Up until that point, Jesus suffered persecution and warned the twelve men He had chosen that they, too, would suffer like persecution due to their chosenness.

> "Remember the words I spoke to you: 'No servant is greater than his master.' If they persecuted me, they will persecute you also. If they obeyed my teaching, they will obey yours also. They will treat you this way because of my name, for they do not know the One who sent me ... But this is to fulfill what is written in their Law: 'They hated me without reason.'"
>
> John 15:20–25

Yes, that's true chosenness; it often results in seemingly reasonless hatred and bitter rejection. Isaiah poignantly described it this way:

> He was despised and rejected by men, a man of sorrows, and familiar with suffering. Like one from whom men hide their faces he was despised, and we esteemed him not. Surely, he took up our infirmities and carried our sorrows, yet we considered him stricken by God, smitten by him, and afflicted.
>
> Isaiah 53:3–4

Oh, the agony of chosenness! It took our Savior to Gethsemane and then on to Calvary.

So, in the Garden, Jesus prayed to His Father in great anguish, asking Him, "Father, if you are willing, take this cup from me; yet not my will, but yours be done." Although the Scripture does not say that He cried out, I know He truly travailed because we know that it is written He sweated drops of blood. Often, I have been reminded of the similarity such an experience is to a mother in the delivery of her child. I have known women to push hard and scream aloud to such an extent that small blood vessels in their eyes and face burst. Then, after having prayed a second time, Jesus yielded Himself to the Father's will by becoming obedient unto death.

Jesus, being both the Passover Lamb (that was to be slain by the head of the Jewish household in each dwelling place) and the scapegoat of Yom Kippur, had to be sacrificed for the human race by a priestly people. The lamb chosen for the Passover sacrifice had to be chosen days in advance and taken into the home for inspection. He had to be a lamb without spot or defect. Jesus was brought into the home of the whole Sanhedrin and the high priest to be examined, and no evidence was found against Him. But when questioned about his Messiahship, He declared Himself to be God (Matthew 26:59–67). The high priest tore his robes, and the Sanhedrin pronounced the sentence of death on Jesus. In their understanding, Jesus spoke blasphemy, and this was punishable by death according to Jewish law.

During and after Jesus's arrest and trial, He was mocked, scourged, sentenced, and then hung on a tree. "He was led like a sheep to the slaughter, and as a lamb before the shearer is silent, so he did not open his mouth" (Acts 8:32). However, recorded for us in the gospels are the cries that went up from Him to the Father while He hung on the cross. In His pain and agony, Jesus "cried out in a loud voice, 'Eloi, Eloi, lama sabachthani?'—which means, 'My God, My God, why have you forsaken me?'" (Matthew 27:46; Mark 15:34). How unthinkable a cry—that, as Martin Luther is said to have said, "God would forsake God." What a concept? But we may have in our very own experience and the Jewish people historically have in their experience that common human condition of utter forsakenness—that we feel as though God, Himself, has abandoned us. That was Jesus's cry. He could not and did not contain it but let it out and let it out loudly.

The second cry we read in the gospels is Messiah's final cry, but oh, what a cry?! For with it, the veil in the temple was torn in two: "And when Jesus had cried out again in a loud voice, he gave up his spirit. At that moment the curtain of the temple was torn in two from top to bottom" (Matthew 27:50–51; Mark 15:37–38). Thus, symbolically, and factually, mankind was given access to enter beyond the veil—to approach God's throne "with boldness." That's a cry, dear reader!

In three days, we know Jesus rose from the dead. The "firstborn over all creation," as Paul calls Him in Colossians 1:15, became the "firstborn from the dead," as John called Him in Revelation 1:5. So even today, Jesus is the "firstfruits of those who have fallen asleep" (I Corinthians 15:20).

Then, Who Killed Jesus?

There is a controversial film, "The Passion of Christ" which was released some time ago that has provoked much criticism. Many feared that this film would unleash a whole new wave of anti-Semitism as some felt like Mel Gibson portrayed Jews in a bad light. The critics felt that too much blame was placed on the Jews for killing Jesus. So the age old question is stirred up once again, "Who killed Jesus?" God's ways are beyond finding out. Who can fathom the mystery of God's sovereignty and the free will of man? Romans 9 wrestles with this issue and uses strong language. God is said to have hardened Pharaoh's heart and God is said to have the right to have mercy on whom He wants to have mercy and to harden those whom He wants to harden. We are told that even our desire for God comes from Him. This being the case, how can God blame us for wrong actions? We are left with an unsatisfying answer, "But who are you to talk back to God?"

Given this dilemma, we are left with vagueness as to who killed Jesus. We have it written in Revelation 13:8, that Jesus was the Lamb that was slain from the creation of the world. In Jesus's own words, we are told that no man had the power to take His life unless it was given to Him from above. In Isaiah 53:10, it says that it was the Lord's will to crush Him and cause Him to suffer. The following Scripture, Acts 4:27–28, highlights this foreordained event. "Indeed Herod and Pontius Pilate met together with the Gentiles and the people of Israel in this city to conspire against your holy servant Jesus, who you anointed. *They did what your power and will had decided beforehand should happen*." God knew from the beginning what it would cost Him to give man a freewill. So I guess we can say that Satan took Jesus's life, or the Jews took his life, or maybe it was the Romans who were the actual ones who tortured and crucified him. When it comes right down to it, God gave His only Son to be atonement for all of our sins. "For God so loved the world that he gave his only begotten son…" (John 3:16). Also, Jesus willingly laid down His life and submitted His will to the will of His Father.

Yet in spite of this truth, the Jewish race has born the guilt of being the ones who killed Jesus. Therefore, ignorant, misinformed people distort this belief to persecute the Jews in each generation. Actually, God is the one who has allowed this chosen race to be among those who fill up the suffering that is lacking in Jesus (in the sense spoken of by the Apostle Paul: "Now I rejoice in what was suffered for you, and I fill up in my flesh what is still lacking in regard to Christ's afflictions, for the sake of his body, which is the church [Colossians 1:24]). Their suffering still has a value in releasing salvation for the world. If their rejection means salvation for the world, what will their acceptance bring (Romans 11)? Hardness has happened in part to the Jewish race so that salvation may come to the Gentiles. Yes, Israel has sinned and deserves to suffer the consequences of her actions, but even her fallenness has a divine purpose—the salvation of the world! It is simplistic to just attribute the persecutions of the Jews in terms of their disobedience, as God has bound us all over to disobedience that He might have mercy on us all.

All this digression is for the purpose of humbling us in our judgments. It is not wise to pronounce judgment on a person or people group, simplistically blaming them for their actions. Without the hand of God's grace surrounding us, we are all capable of great evil.

Conclusion

Throughout the history of Israel, God uses His people as a rock to cause people to stumble. When Israel fell into idolatry and immorality, it was said that God then raised up a nation to execute His judgment. He stirred up the hearts of people to hate the Jew. Then, when the nation completed the punishment of His people, He raised up Israel or another nation to punish their oppressors. And God uses nations that are more corrupt than Israel to be that rod of discipline in His hands.

Habakkuk complains to God that there is great injustice in his land and much destruction and violence was ever before him. In response, God speaks to Habakkuk saying, "I am raising up the Babylonians, that ruthless and impetuous people" (1:6) to discipline His people. Then Habakkuk complains again to God because He is silent while those more wicked than Israel, swallow up the righteous. It just doesn't seem fair, yet God assures Habakkuk that in due season He will punish the Babylonians for how they treated Israel.

In God's mysterious ways, He has used Israel, His chosen people, to be the means of judging the world with regards to the holiness of His own name. They are like salt on an open wound. Their existence tends to draw out the poison found in the hearts of the wicked. When Israel is disobedient over a period of time, they are forced from their land. In the Diaspora, the Jews eventually become comfortable and have to be "forced" to return to their own land. Again and again, God stirs up the people of the nation housing the Jew, and they begin to persecute and mistreat His chosen people.

Then the nation that fulfilled God's purposes in getting His people to return to their own homeland is punished with various judgments. That nation that mistreats the Jewish people falls from being a world power and is cursed in their economy until the reproach is removed through repentance. God has the power to humble the proud and has the power to raise up the meek. He puts in power those whom He chooses.

Israel has experienced a hardening in part, so that salvation might come to the Gentiles. If their very disobedience is a blessing to the world, what will be the outcome of the fullness of their obedience? (See Romans 11.) Oh, the depths of the riches of the wisdom and knowledge of God, His paths are beyond tracing out. The nations are experiencing God's mercy as a result of Israel's disobedience, but now we are to extend mercy to Israel as a result of God's mercy to us. Our histories are intertwined with this ancient people.

This principle of a few being chosen for the sake of many permeates the history of nations. From a human standpoint, this does not seem fair, but isn't a nation's use of armies operating on the same principle? When a nation goes to war, a chosen few are sent to fight the battle on behalf of the whole. Only a small proportion of the population dies for the sake of a better life for those who remain. A few suffer so that others might live. God can be trusted as He is always working towards life, much in the same way as we view doctors. Doctors take an oath to commit themselves to the saving of lives. We believe that most doctors are out for good, so we submit to even the pain they inflict because we are convinced they want us to have a better life … to live!

Jesus was said to be the firstfruits offering and was declared to be the firstfruits of those who would be raised from the dead. He experienced death for all who have sinned so that all who believe might be set free from the fear of death since we are assured of resurrection and everlasting life. Then, we who believe are a kind of firstfruits of all He created (James 1:18).

Through the blood of the sacrificed Lamb, those who were afar off have been drawn close; those who were not a nation have become a nation of royal priests and have been grafted into the olive tree as wild branches. We have come to share in the promises given to Abraham, the father of all who believe! More will be said of this priestly privilege given to those who have come to faith from the nations. God's purpose is to bring everyone to repentance as He is not willing that any should perish. He is preparing a Bride for His Son from among all His people.

THE CRY FOR THE COMING OF HIS GLORIOUS KINGDOM

There is a structure in the center of Old Jerusalem called the Wailing Wall. Hundreds of Jewish men and women go there to pray daily—and not just Jews in the land but those who come from all over the world on a pilgrimage to pay homage to what is left of the temple. The wall is a remote remnant reminding them of the glory that was once theirs. It is a symbol of the days when God reigned in their midst and defeated their enemies. Rivers of tears have been shed there through the centuries from those grieving the loss of this glory, the presence of God. They connect this great tragedy to their own personal losses and suffering. Of course, not all Jews who come here are Jews that believe in God, as absurd as this may seem. But for most, *standing at the wall releases the longing in their hearts for the glorious Kingdom to be restored to them. They cry out for that time where there will be no more sorrow and no more tears.* Most who come to this wall write a prayer request on a piece of paper, fold it into a small piece, and then stick it in one of the numerous spaces between the massive hewn stone building blocks. I have even tucked away a couple of my own prayers in one of those ancient crevices. Many scraps of paper are placed there each year so that periodically the requests are taken down. These spaces become so crammed with paper that many slips fall to the ground and new spaces need to be created.

Each time I visit this sight, I sense a lingering feeling of holiness or presence. This probably is similar to the places where revival broke out in the past like Azusa Street or Herrnhut, Germany, under the Moravians where there was continuous twenty-four seven prayer for over one hundred years. Just think of it, at the Wailing Wall there has been intermittent prayer and tears going up from this site for almost three thousand years! And think of the actual presence of the glory of God resident in the holy of holies in the temple. I would definitely say that this a holy place to visit.

Yes, there were several hundred years of glorious history where the Jewish people experienced the favor of God through His mighty acts. We can read of the faithfulness of Abraham in leaving his own country and going to a place that was foreign to him. We marvel at his courage to take the son of promise, Isaac, and his willingness to even sacrifice him when God required this of him. The stories of Jacob and Joseph in Egypt fascinate and intrigue us, but nothing can be compared to the story of God's awesome deliverance of His people from Egypt! Through a display of power, God released plagues on the Egyptians to force the hand of Pharaoh to let His people go. We read of the final plague, the death of all the firstborn of both man and beast, which finally caused Pharaoh to release the people of God. The Israelites, who obeyed God's instructions to kill a lamb and to put its blood upon the doorpost of their houses, were spared.

Then, perhaps the greatest story of all history occurred when Pharaoh came after the Israelites who were fleeing Egypt. With the fierce armies of their oppressors on one side and the Red Sea on the other, the Israelites once again found themselves in an impossible situation. Moses cried out to God, and the sea parted! Who ever heard of such a thing? And if this wasn't enough to cause fear and trembling in the hearts of the enemies of God, Pharaoh dared to go into the sea bed after the Israelites. But in the perfect timing of the Lord, just as the Israelites made it through to the other side, God caused the waters to come crashing down upon the heads of the horses and chariots, and the enemies of Israel, were drowned.

This one event had such an impact on the neighboring countries that the effects were felt even forty years later when the Israelites prepared to cross into the promised land. News of God's mighty acts on behalf of His people reached the ears of Rahab, the harlot who aided the two spies who came to scout out Jericho.

> I know that the LORD has given this land to you and that a great fear of you has fallen on us, so that all

who live in this country are melting in fear because of you. We have heard how the LORD dried up the water of the Red Sea for you when you came out of Egypt, and what you did to Sihon and Og, the two kings of the Amorites east of the Jordan, whom you completely destroyed. When we heard of it, our hearts melted and everyone's courage failed because of you, for the LORD your God is God in heaven above and on the earth below.

Joshua 2:9–11

Forty years later, this mighty act of God was remembered, and they didn't even have movies, books, or other kinds of media to replay this history! God gave His people a feast, Passover, to celebrate this wonderful event every year. It is an event that God intended to never be forgotten. Even on Shabbat, there are prayers and liturgy commemorating Israel's deliverance from bondage. God's dealings with His people are definitely noteworthy! In Deuteronomy, God reminds us of the uniqueness of the history of His people.

Ask now about the former days, long before your time, from the day God created man on the earth; ask from one end of the heavens to the other. Has anything so great as this ever happened, or has anything like it ever been heard of? Has any other people heard the voice of God speaking out of fire, as you have, and lived? Has any god ever tried to take for himself one nation out of another nation, by testings, by miraculous signs and wonders, by war, by a mighty hand and an outstretched arm, or by great and awesome deeds, like all the things the LORD your God did for you in Egypt before your very eyes? You were shown these things so that you might know that the LORD is God; besides him there is no other. From heaven he made you hear his voice to discipline you. On earth he showed you his great fire, and you heard his words from out of the fire. Because he loved your forefathers and chose their descendants after them, he brought you out of Egypt by his Presence and his great strength, to drive out before you nations greater and stronger than you and to bring you into their land to give it to you for your inheritance, as it is today. Acknowledge and take to heart this day that the LORD is God in heaven above and on the earth below. There is no other.

Deuteronomy 4:32–39

The Israelites enjoyed the very presence of the glory of God while they wandered through the desert. God manifested Himself in a pillar of fire by night and a cloud by day. Time and time again, He showed Himself mighty through His daily provision of food and water. We are told that their very clothes did not wear out during their entire sojourn in the desert. All this happened so that they would not forget the Lord their Maker. *Israel's ongoing favor with God is intimately connected with their presence in their homeland. So to be exiled is a very shameful thing.*

Once you have experienced the mark of favor, the glorious presence of the King, you are forever ruined. Moses cried out to experience more glory and was not content to just have an angel of the LORD attend them in the desert. He wanted God's very presence, or he was not willing to move on. You see, he had spent days on top of the mountain already, speaking face to face with God. He had experienced the lightening and earthquake and the loud thundering voice from heaven. Moses experienced God's greatness and awesome power, yet he wanted more! *Thus, in desperation, he cried out for more of God's glory to empower him to lead his people through the desert. We are told that God answered his prayer and revealed His character to Moses in a fuller measure. God's character of goodness and loving kindness were defined as His glory.*

Moses worshipped in the presence of God and received wisdom for governing, strength for ministering, and power for transformation. When he came out from the tent of meeting, his face glowed with the glory of God, and even his hair turned white! So many times, the writers of Scripture are at a loss for words when it came to describing the glory of God. Perhaps the best way they could explain it was by describing the effect it had on people. When the tabernacle was completed exactly according to the plans God gave Moses, we are told that the glory of the Lord filled the temple and the priests could not stand to minister. Then, when Aaron's two sons offered unauthorized fire before the Lord (only the High Priest was allowed this privilege), fire came out from the presence of the Lord and consumed them. Talk about learning the fear of the Lord the hard way!

When we read the account of Eli in the book of I Samuel, we can get a glimpse of the importance of the glory of God to Israel. When Eli heard about the death of his two sons in the battle against the Philistines he was not as deeply affected as when he heard that the Ark of the Lord, representing the glory of Israel, was captured. He immediately fell over backwards in his chair and died. Then, his daughter-in-law, upon hearing the news of the ark being captured, at once gave birth and with her dying breath she called her son Ichabod, saying "the glory is departed from Israel." When the Ark was returned to them by the Philistines, it remained at Kirjath Jearim for twenty years. During this time, the Israelites lamented after the LORD concerning the Ark.

During David's kingship, he yearned for the presence of God, which the Ark represented, to be in Jerusalem with him. It was said that God dwelt between the cherubim, where His name was proclaimed. David pitched a tent to house the Ark and then made preparations for its return. However, he did not seek the Lord as to how the Ark was to be brought back and had it carried on an oxen cart. When the oxen stumbled and the Ark was in danger of falling, Uzzah, one of the men who was walking alongside the cart, put out his hand to steady the cart. God's anger burned against him, and immediately he was struck dead. David became angry at God saying, "How can I bring the Ark of God to me?" Later, when David consulted the Lord, he found out that he did not do it the right way. Only the Levites were allowed to carry the Ark of the Lord on their shoulders in the prescribed manner.

After the completion of Solomon's temple, we once again read of the weight of glory coming into the completed building and filling the place as a cloud. The priests could not minister and fell on their faces in worship. Thousands of animals were sacrificed in thanksgiving for God's faithfulness, and the temple was dedicated to be the everlasting dwelling place of God. In response to Solomon's plea for God's favor to be upon this temple, the Lord responded.

> When Solomon had finished the temple of the LORD and the royal palace, and had succeeded in carrying out all he had in mind to do in the temple of the LORD and in his own palace, the LORD appeared to him at night and said: I have heard your prayer and have chosen this place for myself as a temple for sacrifices. When I shut up the heavens so that there is no rain, or command locusts to devour the land or send a plague among my people, if my people, who are called by my name, will humble themselves and pray and seek my face and turn from their wicked ways, then will I hear from heaven and will forgive their sin and will heal their land. Now my eyes will be open and my ears attentive to the prayers offered in this place. I have chosen and consecrated this temple so that my Name may be there forever. My eyes and my heart will always be there.
>
> 2 Chronicles 7:11–16

In 2 Chronicles verses 24 to 29, Solomon pleads with God to hear and answer the prayers of His people even if they prayed with hands lifted up towards this temple from a distant place. He foresaw a time when His people would disobey God, and would be forced to leave their land. He even pleaded for the same favor for foreigners who would lift up their prayers towards the temple (2 Chronicles 6:32–33).

There was a period in Solomon's life where the news of the splendor of his glorious kingdom spread far and wide. The queen of Sheba came to Jerusalem to test

Solomon's wisdom and see for herself if the reports of Solomon's greatness were true. This is what she said:

> She said to the king, The report I heard in my own country about your achievements and your wisdom is true. But I did not believe what they said until I came and saw with my own eyes. Indeed, not even half the greatness of your wisdom was told me; you have far exceeded the report I heard. How happy your men must be! How happy your officials, who continually stand before you and hear your wisdom!
>
> 2 Chronicles 9:5–7

King Solomon was greater in riches and wisdom than all the other kings of the earth. All the kings of the earth sought audience with Solomon to hear the wisdom God had put in his heart (2 Chronicles 9:22–23).

Can you imagine the glorious privilege of a nation to house the presence of the Lord? For centuries, the priests faithfully performed their duties of worship in song, prayer, and sacrifice. However, compromises with the world slowly began to affect the purity of their worship, and God brought judgment on them through the hands of the surrounding nations.

There seemed to be a tug of war between the sons of darkness with the sons of light concerning the worship on the temple mount in Jerusalem. As long as Israel was faithful to her God, she maintained possession of the temple, but when she went into idolatry and immorality, the temple was desecrated. Finally, the sin was so great that God enslaved His people in Babylon for seventy years. During the season right before the judgment and during the season of scattering, many Scriptures were written expressing the grief and anguish over the loss of glory.

We can only imagine the grief that Ezekiel must have felt when he saw the glory of God depart from the temple and from Israel itself. "Then the glory of the LORD rose from above the cherubim and moved to the threshold of the temple. The cloud filled the temple and the court was full of the radiance of the glory of the LORD" (Ezekiel 10:4; see verses 1–22). From the threshold, the cherubim departed from the temple, and eventually went from above the city and stopped above a mountain east of it. Then Ezekiel was brought to the exiles in Babylonia, and God gave him words to speak to His people, words of judgment, and words of encouragement. Though they would be exiled from their land, they would return, and He would give them an undivided heart and put a new spirit in them (Ezekiel 11:18–20). The temple would be desecrated, yet God would return to His people, and the temple would be restored. According to Haggai, the glory of the later temple will be greater than the former!

After seventy years of exile—through the decrees of Cyrus, Darius, and Artaxerxes, all kings of Persia, and the preaching of Haggai the prophet and Zechariah the priest—the rebuilding of temple took place. However, the return of the Jewish people to their homeland was not complete, and the glory of the LORD did not return and take up residence in the restored temple. In Ezra 3:11–12, we read of how many of the older priests and Levites and family heads, who had seen the former temple and its glory, wept as they compared the grandeur of the old with the new. Others shouted for joy, perhaps those who had not seen the old temple. Therefore, we have yet to see the greater glory spoken about in the books of Haggai and Ezekiel. Will there be a third temple? Or is the temple referred to a temple made of living stones, those who are of the faith of Abraham in each generation?

Ultimately, the cry in the heart of a Jew over their loss of glory is like the cry that Jesus uttered before his death on the cross: "My God, My God, why have You forsaken Me?" The only real death is separation from God. When our son Samuel died, we experienced the pain of separation; an indescribable gut-wrenching agony as we felt part of our very being was ripped from us. Yet, we know that he is not dead but alive to God. One day, we will see him again. *The Jew's being separated from the favor of God (Oh God, may your face shine upon us and restore our temple as in days of old!) is experienced as a grief like unto death. Until there is a restoration of sonship, there will forever be restlessness in the heart of a Jew.* Coming home is more than coming home to their land. When God heals their hearts from their wounds, their souls will find rest once again in the arms of their loving Father.

Loss of home, loss of glory … and so they wail. Hear the words of their prayer book, the Siddur. On the Sabbath and each Jewish holiday, every observant Jew prays and cries out to God. In earnest they pray, "Be favorable, Hashem, our God toward your people Israel and hear their prayer. Restore the service to the Holy of Holies of Your temple … May the service of Your people be favorable to You" [prayed standing up as part of the Amidah, a series of 18 blessings and requests]. Then a prayer is spoken saying, "May it be your will, Hashem, our God, and the God of our forefathers, that the Holy Temple be rebuilt in our days."

During the celebration of their eight-day festival, Succoth, the intensity of their cry strengthens. These prayers were written during their exile from their land, and many were written in the midst of their suffering among the nations where they lived. So, when they cried out for salvation, it wasn't so that they could be assured a ticket to heaven, as they already believed they had eternal life. *What they cried for was deliverance from their enemies, and for their Kingdom to be restored to them. They were looking forward to the fulfillment of the prophets where the Messiah would come and set up on earth His Kingdom and the nations would beat their swords into plowshares. They were looking for a new heaven and new earth where the lion would lie down with the lamb and the bear would eat grass like the ox. The creation itself would be redeemed from accursedness.*

Recently, I met with an old friend whom I haven't seen for many months. I was shocked to see that all his hair had turned a pure white. He looked twenty years older. He went on to explain that he had some kind of auto-immune disease that knocked out all his hair. Then, when it grew back, it came back all white. I felt a sense of grief or sorrow as I perceived a diminishing of glory as this was not how I remembered him. In much the same way, within the Jewish DNA, there is a remembrance of former glory, and there is yet a corporate cry and grief that is being unleashed. *One day, when God releases the spirit of grace and supplication upon them, they will look upon Him whom they have pierced. They will see that the glory they were seeking in the coming of their victorious Messiah, who would set up His Kingdom, was actually the one they rejected. They will see that He was the glory throughout their history all along.* He was the Angel that spoke to Abraham; He was the Angel that revealed Himself to Moses, and the Angel that accompanied their ancestors through the wilderness. The floodgates of centuries of tears will be released, and they will weep and wail as if they were mourning over the loss of their firstborn son. Then, their eyes will be opened, and they will understand that Jesus is their Redeemer. The fountain of cleansing will burst forth and cleanse them from all their sin. The prodigal will come to his senses and acknowledge that all the ways of God are just and true. They will come home at last, and no one will be able to pluck them from their land again!

Conclusion

God has produced and is producing an intercessory people among the Jews that has and will continue to stand in the gap and cry out for mercy. They have been kept as a people who cannot put down roots, a people who have suffered many losses. They are not allowed to get too comfortable as the longing for the kingdom has to remain fresh in their hearts. For their entire history as a people, they had to see and experience the life of a sojourner. As Abraham was moved out of his comfort zone when God asked him to leave his country and family, he was put in a place of constant dependency on God, so too his descendants.

The book of Hebrews, chapter 11, reports the stories of many great men and women of faith whose lives were patterned after the life of Abraham.

> By faith Abraham, when called to go to a place he would later receive as his inheritance, obeyed and went, even though he did not know where he was going. By faith he made his home in the promised land like a stranger in a foreign country; he lived in tents, as did Isaac and Jacob, who were heirs with him of the same promise. For he was looking forward to the city with foundations, whose architect and builder is God.
>
> Hebrews 11:8–10

> All these people were still living by faith when they died. They did not receive the things promised; they only saw them and welcomed them from a distance. And they admitted that they were aliens and strangers on earth. People who say such things show that they are looking for a country of their own.
>
> Hebrews 11:13–14

During the Diaspora, the Jew often would settle down in his new country. Because of his diligence and divine gifting, he prospered wherever he went. In order for God to fulfill His promises concerning His people returning to their own land, He has had to repeatedly cause the nation in which they have settled to vomit them from their midst. In Germany, many Jews were warned of the pending danger but refused to leave as they had become comfortable. How true this principle for us today. When we get too comfortable with life in this world as it is, we become complacent and are content to live a life void of Kingdom reality. We lose our ability to see the unseen and seek comfort and provision through the arm of the flesh. *However, God wants us to continually cry out for His Kingdom manifestation on earth and to look to Him as our source of strength and provision. Hence, we have a first fruits people group going on ahead, forever being put out of their "homeland" so that they will cry out to their God for provision and for deliverance.*

THE CRY OF THE WESTERN CHURCH

Many years ago, in the mid 1960s, our country went through a crisis involving Cuba and the threat of a nuclear attack. I can remember that there was great fear of another world war, and many people had bomb shelters dug into the ground near their houses. Since we came from a fundamentalist Baptist church, our family believed that we would be raptured out of here before the tribulations came upon the earth. Therefore, we did not have to be concerned about a nuclear threat. The eschatological theology of the day seemed to be that of escapism; rather than seeing God's Kingdom established on the earth, the Western Church of that time looked to escape the corruption on planet earth. Our goal was to go to heaven rather than bring heaven to earth.

This view stood in direct contrast to the Jewish view of seeking a kingdom manifestation on earth. The Jewish people were looking for peace to come to earth and a transformation of creation where the lion would lay down with the lamb and the bear would eat grass like the ox. The prophets foresaw a kingdom where there would be no more war, where their swords would be beaten into plowshares. While *The Cry* from many belonging to the Western Church during this period was, "Come Lord Jesus and get me out of here," *The Cry* of the Jew was, "May Your Kingdom come on earth as it is in heaven."

Heaven for the Jew was a transformed life on earth through the presence of the Holy Spirit, the glory of God. Prophets foretold a day where the glory of the Lord would fill the earth as the waters covered the beds of the sea. This theology can be clearly seen in the story of the disciples walking with Jesus on the road to Emmaus. They did not recognize Jesus as being the one walking with them as they were expecting a victorious Messiah who would bring the kingdom of heaven to earth. They were looking for a Messiah that would redeem Israel from her enemies.

Their history is replete with stories of God's delivering them from their enemies and restoring the kingdom to them. It took Jesus's explaining the Old Covenant Scripture to them concerning the necessity for the Messiah's coming first to suffer and die and then coming a second time to restore the kingdom. This idea that His Kingdom was to come by Jesus forcing His rule upon the world was still ingrained in their thinking up until the time of Jesus's ascension. At that time, His disciples asked if Jesus was going to restore the kingdom to Israel right then. Jesus never rebuked them for their theology but said that it was not for them to know the time nor the season of this restoration.

John the Baptist even doubted the Messiahship of Jesus because he was in prison, and it appeared to him that things were getting worse rather than better. According to his understanding, the coming of the Messiah would bring world peace, the Roman oppressors would be overthrown, and God would set up His government in Jerusalem. Israel would be chief among the nations. What was happening to John did not compute with his theology. Jesus had to send back John's disciples declaring that indeed He was the One because the blind had received their sight, the lame walked, the dead were raised, and the good news was preached to the poor. What Jesus was talking about was the kingdom manifestation of His rule on earth. Where the dominion of the King was in operation, Satan's kingdom retreated. Sickness, poverty, death, etc. had to flee in the presence of the King, as these things are not found in heaven.

So where is the Kingdom today? Why aren't we seeing more miracles in the Church in America and in other modern nations? I believe it is because we have become too comfortable in life. Many of us are living in exile and do not even realize it. We are living in our own Diaspora. We find we have no need for our Creator because we can do everything for ourselves. We have good doctors and medicine; we have credit cards; we have good methods of healing the emotionally sick; we have plenty of money to buy things; we have good schools and excellent books; and we have made brilliant technological and scientific discoveries.

I believe all of this has made the Western Church so independent that these things appear to displace God. Even church life goes on in many places with no recognition that God's presence is not among them. There is still a remnant, however, of people within the Church who acknowledge their utter dependence on God. Why only a remnant? Could it be because only those who are aware of their needs and their own powerlessness to solve their problems will recognize God? "Blessed are the poor in spirit, for theirs is the kingdom of heaven" (Matthew 5:3).

In the parable of the four soils, we read of the tragedy of the seeds sown among the thorns. It is one of the parables of the kingdom that Jesus told to his disciples. To summarize, the seed that falls among thorns represents the Word of God being sown in the hearts of those who have received the good news of the Kingdom and perhaps have walked in victory for a while, but then they became distracted. Their hearts became weighed down through their concern for material possessions, worry, and a seeking after pleasure. In these hearts, the fruitfulness of the kingdom was blocked as the cares of this life choked the word. These people became friends of the world, and had lost sight of the unseen; the eternal Kingdom. They might have even stopped longing for it, as many in this category do not even realize that they are poor, pitiful, and naked. There is little or no recognition that the "glory" has left. They have no "wailing wall" of remembrance and, therefore, do not mourn over the loss of the glory of the kingdom of God. They are comfortable and do not need the supernatural. Their conscience has become singed, and the shock over the recognition of sin is no longer present. How long will God allow this complacency to go on?

In China, the believers do not get a chance to get "comfortable" in this life. Therefore, they are constantly crying out to God for more grace, provision, or deliverance. Many signs and wonders are done in their midst. They know that without God's intervention there is no hope for them. The Kingdom of God is so real to them, more real and valuable than their lives in this world, that they are willing to lose everything in order to gain the Kingdom! *A desperate people obtain supernatural intervention!* Out of great suffering a people committed to the purposes of God connect to the groaning of all creation and cry out as a woman in labor for God's Kingdom to be manifest in their lives, in their families, or in their cities and nations. Why is it usually only out of pain that we cry out?

Yes, we will have a shaking in America. Indeed, it has already started. *Though there isn't a physical promised land like Israel, we are to return to that which God promised us. He has promised us the Kingdom—a place where His will is done. Let us long for the establishment of His government.* When His government manifests on this earth, then there will be peace in all our spheres of life. It is a kingdom that cannot be shaken, and we are told that in the last days everything that is not part of this kingdom will be removed. Everything that is not eternal in composition will fall away. Only that which is birthed through the incorruptible seed will survive. But Hebrews 12 says that this is an occasion to rejoice in that our Kingdom will never pass away. Seek first His kingdom and His righteousness, and everything else will fall into place!

When the Book of the Law was found in the Temple by Hilkiah the high priest, he brought it to Josiah, king of Judah. Shaphan, the secretary to the king, then read from the Law to Josiah, and his heart was smitten. He tore his robes in horror as he realized the implications of the words of this book. Within this book, God expounded the Law given to Moses and the curses that would come upon Israel if they disobeyed (2 Kings 22:8–20). Because Josiah's heart was responsive to the word and he humbled himself before the Lord through weeping, God declared that He would spare his experiencing the judgment that He was going to release upon the Israelites.

Let us pray for the spirit of grace and supplication to come upon His Church that we may wake up from our slumber and recognize our nakedness and need. We are without our glory clothes and desperately need to be covered with His glory once again. It is time for the Church to arise and shine. It is time to cry out and break up our hard hearts until He showers righteousness on us. We must not give up until He comes. Let us erect our own wailing wall of remembrance and not allow ourselves to be satisfied until the full manifestation of His Kingdom comes in power. We are in a battle that we cannot win without the power of God through his Holy Spirit. The salvation of Israel depends on the Church's having sufficient kingdom manifestation to make Israel jealous. (See Romans 11.)

Where the church is flourishing, many Jews come to faith. When signs of God's favor rests on the believers from among the nations, there will be enough power to release the Jews from their unbelief. The salvation of

Israel depends on the Gentiles, and the salvation of the Gentiles depends upon prayers and obedience of God's chosen people, Israel. God has so artistically intertwined our two destinies. *Rise up, oh Church, and cry out to God for His Kingdom to come on earth. Cry out to God for Israel to be resurrected from the dead so that there will be manifest on earth the glory of God for all to see.*

THE CRY FOR THE SALVATION OF ALL

God, in His wisdom, ordained that the Jews and the Gentiles would have a mutually interdependent relationship of blessing. Neither one will come into their inheritance, their destiny, without the other. Therefore, it is crucial to understand the season we are in so we know where to direct our prayers and energy, remembering God's heart is for all to come to salvation. All that He does has this as His goal. So when we pray for Israel it is so that she can do her part in bringing salvation to the nations, and when we pray for the believers among the nations, we are praying for them to be filled with the glory of God so that Israel will be made jealous.

In this chapter, we will look at the nature of *The Cry* that will arise from among the nations for the salvation of Israel. In the last chapter, we will get a glimpse of what God is preparing in the heart of the Jew to release grace for the nations in the last days.

Romans 11 warns that the wild branches, those who are from among the nations, should not boast against the natural branches that have been cut off. Israel's hardness is temporary until the full number of Gentiles comes to salvation. Branches were broken off so that salvation could come to the Gentiles, how easy it will be for God to graft back in the natural olive branches. *To have a concern for the salvation of Israel is to have a concern for world redemption and for the Church to come to her full place of glory. Since Israel's disobedience brought grace for salvation for the Gentiles, how much greater riches will their fullness bring?* Can we even imagine what those greater riches are? Life from the dead is promised to be the final outcome of Israel's restoration.

I believe that we are living in critical times, a *kairos* moment. We are on the brink of something great. For two thousand years, God preserved the human race through the obedience of the faithful Israelites who performed daily services in the temple on behalf of their people and on behalf of the nations. Yet, they were not successful in bringing world redemption. Now, we are at the end of two thousand years of Church history where even with the power of the Holy Spirit, we have not brought the world to redemption. We have yet to see a city or nation, or people group, consistently walk out obedience to God and His law, sufficient to transform the area where they live. The blessings for obedience given to Israel as a nation and to those who are of the spiritual seed of Abraham have not been fully manifested.

Even in China, where perhaps the greatest manifestation of God's glory exists, there are still miscarriages. The enemies of God are still allowed to continue their evil, and prosperity still has not been the condition of the land. Has the Church fulfilled her great commission? No. Neither Israel nor the Church has been able to bring salvation to the ends of the earth as it is today. Though individuals have come to that place of holiness and righteousness, there is no city or nation in the world that carries the torch for all to see kingdom reality.

Our daughter, Simcha, when she was in the Israeli army, had many opportunities to share her faith with fellow soldiers. Many times the topic came around to her personal life of purity. She would tell them that she believed in the principal of courtship instead of dating. Simcha had agreed to place the affections of her heart under her father's loving protection until her father deemed that she was mature enough and ready to get married. She had chosen to not let her heart out to any other man until her father released her. Therefore, she had never dated and has never had a boyfriend, though many men pursued her. Often, she was confronted by these soldiers, both male and female, with today's lie that an individual should have sex prior to marriage so as to discover if there was sexual compatibility with the partner. No matter how hard she tried to explain the holiness of sex and her views of saving herself for marriage, they did not comprehend her abstinence.

This blindness and hardness of heart, in a people group that is supposed to represent the holiness of God to the nations, grieved our daughter. It appeared that this immorality was the stumbling block hindering her fellow soldiers from coming to faith. Somehow, they knew that if they yielded to God, then they would no longer be able to engage in their licentious lifestyle. The truth of the following Scripture becomes clear:

> They are darkened in their understanding and separated from the life of God because of the ignorance that is in them due to the hardening of their hearts. Having lost all sensitivity, they have given themselves over to sensuality so as to indulge in every kind of impurity, with a continual lust for more.
>
> Ephesians 4:18–19

So, in Israel, we have two extremes of unsaved Jews. There are those of the super-religious sects of Judaism that are bound by legalism with an anti-Messiah inclination, and then there are those who are secular Jews that have thrown off all restraint. These react to anything that smells of Orthodoxy or religion. And members from both groups have become hardened by the great suffering, persecution, and holocausts of their people. We need to cry out to God to break through this hardness so they will turn and be healed. Scripture says a veil covers their hearts so they cannot see the light of the gospel of the glory of Christ, who is the image of God (2 Corinthians 4:4).

Sometimes, the ground of people's hearts seems so hard. The good news of the Gospel doesn't seem to be able to penetrate. Many soldiers do not believe that faith in God can be as pleasurable as sex. It is not their "Jewishness" that trips them up, as is the case with the religious Jews, but their unbelief in the goodness of God. How grateful I am for the promises of God's word and the power of the Holy Spirit for breaking up this fallow ground. We need to ask God for His mercy and grace to come upon His intercessors so we will not lose heart in the process of praying for Israel and the nations. There is a danger that in the face of such apparent difficulty, we too, will allow discouragement to kill the flame of passion in our own hearts.

We are now entering into the "third day" (a day being a thousand years) of the Church and have finished the "fourth day" of Jewish history (around 4,000 years since Abraham). Perhaps we are about to experience a double resurrection, a third day resurrection of the Gentile church and a resurrection of the Jewish people like Lazarus who was raised after he had been dead for four days. Since God works with Israel first in releasing more grace, and then releases grace for the believers from among the nations, we can expect that soon there will be greater grace released in Israel. (There are many books explaining in detail the parallel restoration between Israel and the Church.) Can you imagine the power that will be released when the Spirit is poured out in Jerusalem on a group of Jewish believers? *Since we are still waiting for the temple filled with greater glory, spoken about in Haggai, perhaps God is about to pour out His spirit on a temple of living stones right in Jerusalem that will release grace worldwide.*

Ezekiel speaks about a time when the nations will recognize God when He makes His people holy in their midst. (See Ezekiel 36:23–36.) The glory of God fell on the tabernacle of Moses and on the temple of Solomon when everything was completed according to the pattern given to them from God. Perhaps now so much grace will be poured out on Israel that people's lives will be built into conformity to the living temple, Jesus. And then, when there is such purity and holiness of action, the Spirit will descend in great power and glory and release grace all over the world for believers to walk out their obedience. They will become that light shining in a dark place. And nations will come to their light as they see the brightness of a righteousness that comes through faith. God said that He would not rest until He made Jerusalem's righteousness shine out like the dawn. So how should we pray?

We have to face the facts. Israel is seeped in sin right now. Immorality is rampant among the secular Israelis. The women in the army, for example, are allowed three free abortions. Fortunetellers set up their wares in public shopping malls. We are to weep for Israel's heart has become hardened and desensitized to sin (though we see openness to the Gospel increasing). *So we call together the wailing women to cry out like Ezra for the sins of his people.* Perhaps there is some merit or favor coming upon us as we are faithful to cry out for God to cause righteousness and praise to spring up in Israel and among the nations. The Lord said to a man clothed in linen to go throughout the streets of Jerusalem and put a mark on the foreheads of those who grieve and lament over all the detestable things that are done in it. All those who did not have the mark were to be put to death.

"Go throughout the city of Jerusalem and put a mark on the foreheads of those who grieve and lament over all the detestable things that are done in it." As I listened, he said to the others, "Follow him through the city and kill, without showing pity or compassion. Slaughter old men, young men and maidens, women and children, but do not touch anyone who has the mark. Begin at my sanctuary."

Ezekiel 9:4–6

It was the spirit of holiness that raised Jesus from the dead. Perhaps we are poised for a resurrection. God will not rest until "He has made Jerusalem praise in all the earth." He will show Himself holy through her and through the Church. He will have a bride without spot or wrinkle! *Lazarus, come forth! Rise from the dead, oh ye sleeper, and God's glory will shine upon you. Nations will come to your light and the holiness of God's great Name will be redeemed.* No longer will His name be profaned amongst the nations. God chose us in Him before the creation of the world to be holy and blameless in His sight: "For he chose us in him before the creation of the world to be holy and blameless in his sight. In love he predestined us to be adopted as his sons through Jesus Christ, in accordance with his pleasure and will" (Ephesians 1:4–5). His word will prevail! So cry out for the salvation of Israel and the nations of the world.

THE CRY FOR THE RETURN OF JESUS

God is extremely patient and does not quickly pour out His wrath. He allows plenty of time for people to come to repentance and looks for every opportunity to be gracious. However, eventually God has to release judgment in order for righteousness to be learned. Isaiah 26:9–10 says, "When your judgments come upon the earth, the people of the world learn righteousness. Though grace is shown to the wicked, they do not learn righteousness; even in a land of uprightness they go on doing evil and regard not the majesty of the LORD." Such darkness can be unleashed over an area that justice and righteousness seem far removed and truth is nowhere to be found. (See Isaiah 5:14–1.)

God looks for those who will stand in the gap and weep over the sins of the people and call out for mercy.

But when He cannot find that person or people, or the sin of a people becomes so great—"even if Moses and Samuel were to stand before me, my heart would not go out to this people" (Jeremiah 15:1)—His own arm will work salvation. God can be pushed too far, to put it in human terms. Eventually, His wrath is aroused, and there is no remedy. (See 2 Chronicles 36:15–16.) He will clothe Himself with His zeal and will wear the breastplate of righteousness; He will rend the heavens and redeem the holiness of His name.

Yet, even in wrath, He remembers mercy, for mercy triumphs over judgment. Judgment is coming upon the world, but we have this hope—God's compassionate heart. He will sustain us and enable us to endure the troubles in the last days. He will even cut them short for the sake of His elect. May God increase our faith so that our hearts may see the power of our prayers to release God's grace in the midst of judgment.

In Numbers 16:41–50, we can see how first Moses and Aaron intervened when God was ready to pour out His wrath and completely destroy the assembly of Israelites who grumbled again against Moses and Aaron. They fell face down as God began to unleash His fury. They were not able to stay God's hand completely, but their prayers limited the amount of destruction. Only 14,700 people died from the plague that broke out against them. Many more could have perished.

Another example of an individual intervening and limiting the amount of destruction is King David. After he wrongly counted the mighty men of Israel, God unleashed judgment upon the people through a devastating plague. Though David quickly built an altar to the Lord and made atonement through burnt offerings, over 70,000 people died as a result of the plague. God received David's repentance and prayers and stopped the plague.

We have repeated examples of God's intervention in response to the Israelites and their crying out in the midst of judgment. In these incidences, it was not just one person who cried out, but a nation in corporate unity cried out. In Judges, we read of a repeated history of His people where they would slowly allow idolatry and immorality to compromise their loyalty to God. In response to their continued hardening of heart, God would raise up a nation to execute judgment upon His people. Then, they would become oppressed by their enemy for several years. In due time, they would cry out to God, turn from their ways, and God would then raise up a deliverer. Nehemiah 9:26–31 speaks of this pattern:

> But they were disobedient and rebelled against you; they put your law behind their backs. They killed your prophets, who had admonished them in order to turn them back to you; they committed awful blasphemies. So you handed them over to their enemies who oppressed them. But when they were oppressed they cried out to you. From heaven you heard them, and in your great compassion you gave them deliverers, who rescued them from the hand of their enemies. But as soon as they were at rest, they again did what was evil in your sight.

In God's great mercy, He did not completely put an end to them even though they repeated this pattern of disobedience again and again. It seemed like this people could not handle peace and prosperity without it going to their head. Comfort seemed to be their enemy as they easily forgot their Creator and ignored the requirements of His law. We can see that in God's mercy He allowed troubles to stir their hearts anew to seek Him. For God was and is desirous for His people to enter into their destiny of being lights in this world and being a ruling queen by the Jesus's side in the age to come. He wanted them to be able to remain in their homeland.

When God's people became reprobate, He always sent them messengers, prophets, to warn them of impending judgment. Again and again, He pled with them to turn from their wicked ways and always gave them time to repent. Then God would announce the inevitability of judgment when all other attempts failed. When the prophets heard this, they would often rend their garments and weep and wail. Yet, not even their tears could change God's heart when He came to this place.

However, because of God's great compassion, He never talked of judgment without giving the Israelites hope for restoration. He wounds, but He also heals. Hosea 6:1–3 says, "Come let us return to the LORD. He has torn us to pieces but he will heal us; he has injured us but he will bind up our wounds…". Jeremiah 30 speaks for restoration after judgment, "But all who devour you will be devoured; all your enemies will go into exile … but I will restore you to health and heal your wounds, declares the LORD." In the midst of suffering, He brought encouragement that their suffering would only be for a season.

Through endurance and the encouragement of Scriptures, we can have hope. We can learn from the experiences of God's dealings with Israel and understand the times in which we live. We will then know how to direct our prayers. America has been warned by God's messengers again and again. Many have heard their cry and have wept over the sins in their land.

We know that judgment will begin in the household of faith. God will purify the "Levites" first so that they will be able to stand in the gap. With cleanness of heart they will make intercession, first for all those who are of the household of faith and then for the people in their city and nation. I believe we are still at the time of purifying the Church so she will have a legitimate voice to warn the people of the world. A church in self-righteousness will not have sufficient grace to stand in the gap. Through God's great mercy He is increasing our faith and preparing us to be that light shining in dark places. God is faithful and will stay His hand of judgment until He has His army in place with the seal of God upon their foreheads that is spoken of in Revelation 7.

The travail of suffering will be so great that the hearts of many will grow cold. Though ample time will be given to repent, multitudes will enter the next season with ever-increasing hardness of heart. Even though it will be clearly seen that the troubles in the last days are caused by the hand of God, men will curse God and will refuse to repent. (See Revelation 9:20–21; 16:8–11.) There will be last days' Pharaohs whose hearts God will harden so that He may show His great glory as He delivers His saints. We are reminded again and again that during the last days' judgments, we are called to patiently endure. Both the righteous and the unrighteous will suffer but for the righteous God will release abundant grace. Where sin abounds, God's grace will abound all the more.

So, what should be our cry? We cry out for mercy, that the days of trouble be cut short. We cry of for grace to endure and grace to remain faithful until the end. We cry out for the laborer of the harvest to go out with greater power so that salvation would reach the ends of the earth. As God released judgment on the nations who mistreated His people Israel, so God will avenge the blood of those who have suffered for the sake of the gospel. All the tears and prayers of the saints are being kept before His throne and soon there will be a fullness of intercession. God will hear our corporate cry for deliverance and send the Deliverer, the Lion of the Tribe of Judah who triumphs over His foes.

The armies from every nation will be aligned against Israel, and it will look like all hope is gone. Jerusalem will be ransacked again, and it will look like this witness people will be totally annihilated. Yet God has had this day in mind since before the creation of the world. By this time, He will have made His Bride ready. In her is the same glory that is in the Messiah and that glory will have manifested as a divine unity of the people of faith. The Body across the world will have properly positioned herself before the throne of God to cry in intercession. God will have ignited their hearts with love for Israel, a love so intense that it will overpower the raging hatred arrayed against her from the nations.

At that time, we will be like unto a woman about to give birth. We will cry out to God, looking to Him as the only one who can save, and we will receive the supernatural strength to push the baby out. No longer will we fear pain or death, for what will matter most to us is seeing the Kingdom manifested on earth. We want to see our King. The cries of the people from the nations will unite with the prayers of the faithful from among the Jews, and with one voice, we will cry out, "Hosanna, LORD save! Blessed is He who comes in the name of the LORD." And then the trumpet will sound, and the Lord will appear with His army to deliver His people Israel, and then He will save His people—His bride. Every knee will bow and confess that Jesus is Lord. The glory of God will cover the earth as the waters cover the beds of the sea! Let us press on to release this glorious purpose. Jesus in us is the hope of glory. Amen.